Crafting Faith

101 Crafts to Help Kids Grow in Their Faith

Laurine M. Easton

LOYOLA PRESS.
A JESUIT MINISTRY
Chicago

LOYOLA PRESS.
A JESUIT MINISTRY

3441 N. Ashland Avenue
Chicago, Illinois 60657
(800) 621-1008
www.loyolapress.com

This book was put together with the help of many people among whom are Barbara Albin and Julia Holek.

A previous edition of this book was published in 1987 as *Crafts for Religious Education* (ISBN 1-55588-144-0) by TEL Publishers, Ltd, PO Box 5471, Rockford, Illinois 61125.

Scripture texts in this work are taken from the *New American Bible with Revised New Testament and Revised Psalms* © 1991, 1986, 1970 Confraternity of Christian Doctrine, Washington, D.C. and are used by permission of the copyright owner. All Rights Reserved. No part of the *New American Bible* may be reproduced in any form without permission in writing from the copyright owner.

Cover Image: © Keren Su/CORBIS
Cover design: Beth Herman
Interior illustrations: Yoshi Miyake, Mia Basile and Kathryn Seckman Kirsch
Interior design: Mia Basile and Kathryn Seckman Kirsch

Library of Congress Cataloging-in-Publication Data
Easton, Laurine M.
  Crafting faith : 101 crafts to help kids grow in their faith / Laurine M. Easton.
     p. cm.
  Includes index.
  ISBN-13: 978-0-8294-2704-2
  ISBN-10: 0-8294-2704-X
  1. Christian education—Activity programs. 2. Creative activities and seat work.
  3. Christian education of children. I. Title.
  BV1536.E27 2008
  268'.6—dc22

                                                    2008014956

Printed in United States of America

08 09 10 11 12 BANG 10 9 8 7 6 5 4 3 2 1

Contents

Introduction

Did you know that the Bible begins with a craft activity?

The creation stories in the Book of Genesis (chapters 1 and 2) explain to us how, out of the divine imagination, God crafted the heavens and the earth, the stars, the sun, the moon, the oceans, plants, and living creatures, culminating in the crafting of human beings. Simply put, crafting is the art of creating an object with skill and careful attention to detail. Creation is nothing other than God's craftwork. Made in the image and likeness of God, we human beings are driven to create. Crafting is a way of participating in the creative nature of God and in the divine imagination.

Crafting has long held a privileged place in religious education. The making of crafts allows children (as well as people of all ages) to concretely and creatively express their understanding of the faith and of their relationship with God and the Church. Art is a "language" that we use in religious education to "bring the divine to the human world, to the level of the senses, then, from the spiritual insight gained from the senses and the stirring of the emotions, to raise the human world to God, to his inexpressible kingdom of mystery, beauty, and life" (*NDC* 37B1).

Crafting also is an effective teaching method for those whose learning style is not primarily word based. The concept of multiple intelligences—developed by Dr. Howard Gardner, a professor of education at Harvard University—classifies learners according to their particular strengths:

- Linguistic
- Logical-mathematical
- Magic
- Bodily-kinesthetic
- Spatial
- Interpersonal
- Intrapersonal

People who are more comfortable drawing than writing will benefit from opportunities to express themselves through art. Likewise, some people simply learn best when they are invited to do something tactile. These people, known as *haptic* learners because of their tendency to rely on touch as a primary intake source, are often well coordinated and enjoy hands-on activities. Crafting allows those learners who are more visual, artistic, and physical to express themselves and to learn in a manner that more closely fits their learning style. Even for those whose learning style is more word based, crafting offers a change of pace. Learning in general is more effective when a variety of methods is employed and when participants are actively engaged.

Finally, the Catholic faith is fundamentally sacramental; it is a faith that goes beyond words and recognizes God's presence reflected in the things of our world. The Catholic imagination looks to the elements of creation as channels of God's grace. Whether it be the "official" sacramental elements such as water, bread, wine, oil, and fire, or the countless other elements available to us such as rocks, seashells, acorns, pinecones, fabric, paper, flowers, wood, and, yes, even crafting stems, the Catholic capacity for recognizing God in the physical world is unlimited.

And, of course, one more thing . . . *crafting is fun!*

Tips for Using Crafts in Religious Education

1. Well before the beginning of the program year, identify opportunities for using crafts to express visually what you are teaching. List possible projects and materials that you might need for the year. Work with your catechetical leader to acquire materials or ask parents to donate them.

2. Crafting should never take the place of actual teaching. It should be used either to supplement teaching or to provide participants with an outlet to express their understanding of what has been taught.

3. Complete the craft yourself to be more familiar with the time and skill involved. Doing so will also help you to decide how much of the work needs to be prepared in advance in order to allow your students to complete the task within the allotted time. This will also help you to determine the age-appropriateness of the craft project.

4. Before doing a craft, be sure that the concept, theme, or doctrine being taught is clearly understood by all. Then, introduce the craft activity as a way of reinforcing this message or of expressing a response to the teaching. Explain the reason this particular craft has been chosen and how it connects to the lesson.

5. The more complex the craft project, the more helpers or aides you will need to assist the students. Do not assume that the students will be as informed as you are about the steps of the project.

6. Be sure to have all of your materials organized and readily accessible.

7. Provide directions for how to complete the craft project before distributing any materials or inviting the students to leave their places. Check for comprehension by asking for volunteers to summarize the directions in their own words.

8. Look over the space you will be using to avoid and eliminate any unnecessary distractions for the students. If possible, decorate the crafting area in the theme of the project being created. This decoration will provide a visual incentive for the students. It can be as simple as displaying the project that you completed in advance. Other appropriate pictures or symbols can enhance the environment.

9. Consider playing appropriate music that supports the theme of the project and provides a calming effect.

10. Impart a sense of pride in doing the project creatively and with care, telling the students that artistic expression is how God created the heavens and the earth and that when we express ourselves artistically, we participate in God's creative process.

11. Spread newspapers around to cover tabletops and to keep the work area neat and clean.

12. Arrange the students in pairs or small groups at tables with an aide at each table to assist. Have a separate table set up with supplies and materials.

13. Try to use a variety of materials and ideas throughout the year. Give the students freedom to create, options to choose from, and encouragement as they work.

14. Be prepared to keep certain craft projects for drying and so forth until the students return to retrieve the projects later that day or at the next session. Be sure each student has clearly identified which craft project belongs to him or her.

Collage of Signs and Symbols

Grades 1–8

Materials:

Magazines	Scissors
Poster board	Crayons or felt-tip markers
Glue or paste	Drawing Paper

FAITH CONNECTION

Explain to the students that the Church uses signs and symbols to express our faith. Brainstorm a list (water, bread, wine, oil, etc.).

Directions:

1. Have the students move into small groups and make a collage of different signs they see every day. Encourage the students to use some of the signs of the Church as the focal point of their collages.

2. Cut out pictures from magazines or have the students draw their own signs or symbols to cut out and put together on one collage.

3. This project could be a one-day or a two-day project. Draw and cut the first day. Then paste and discuss the different collages the second day.

Note: As an alternative, you could have the students bring their own special-interest magazines.

Felt Bookmarkers

Grades 1–8

Materials:

One 2" × 6" strip of stiff felt for each student	Scissors
Additional colored felt	White glue
Cardboard patterns of symbols (see page 3)	Optional: Trim material such as gold braid, silver and gold thread, embroidery floss and ribbon
Pencils	

Before Class:

Prepare ample cardboard patterns for the students. Cut out felt symbols before class for younger students. They can then arrange and glue the symbol on their bookmarkers. Invite children to decorate their bookmarkers with trim materials.

Directions:

1. Provide a sample bookmarker to help the students proceed with a bookmarker project of their choice. Supply samples or patterns of the symbols.

2. This project can be used for all grade levels, depending upon the complexity of the symbol chosen. Use simple, single-piece patterns for grades 1 and 2.

3. Choose two different colors of felt: one for the bookmarker itself and one for the symbol to be put onto the bookmarker.

4. Choose one of the symbol patterns from page 3 of this book or draw your own Christian symbol.

5. Trace the pattern on a piece of felt. Cut out the symbol.

6. Glue the symbol to the bookmarker.

7. Decorate with scrap pieces of felt and/or trim material.
   Using scissors, cut the bottom of the bookmarker to make fringe

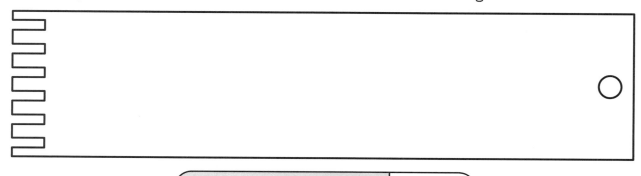

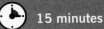

Bookmarkers

Grades 3–8

Materials:

Cardboard patterns of symbols	Felt-tip pens
Lightweight poster board cut into 2" × 6" strips	Paper punch
Colored construction paper	Colored twine, yarn, or ribbon
Crayons	Glue

> **FAITH CONNECTION**
> *Explain to the students that the Church uses signs and symbols to express our faith. Brainstorm a list (water, bread, wine, oil, etc.).*

Before Class:

Prepare cardboard patterns and poster board strips for the students.

Directions:

1. This project may be done by using colored construction paper for the symbols and lightweight poster board for the bookmarkers.

2. Choose one of the symbol patterns and trace it on a piece of construction paper.

3. Glue the symbol onto the poster board bookmarker.

4. Decorate the bookmarker with crayons or felt-tip pens. A Bible verse may be added.

5. Punch a hole near the top and loop a piece of colored twine, yarn, or narrow ribbon through the top of the bookmarker.

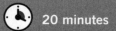 20 minutes

Puzzle Project

Grades 3–8

Materials:

Magazines	White paper
Stiff, non-corrugated cardboard (from pads of paper)	Crayons
Glue	Pencils
Scissors	

FAITH CONNECTION

One important way to understand "Church" is to see it as a community of people. We are the Church, the People of God.

Directions:

1. From a magazine, have each student cut out a picture of groups of people symbolizing community or have each student draw a picture of his or her own family and community with different people in the picture.

2. Glue the pictures to the stiff cardboard. Do not use corrugated cardboard.

3. Turn the cardboard over and draw lines on the back to make a puzzle outline.

4. Cut out the puzzle pieces, following the lines. Students can trade puzzles and work on each other's puzzles.

Walking with the Lord

Grades 1–8

Materials:

Construction paper, poster board, or cardstock	Scissors
Pencils, crayons, or markers	Masking tape

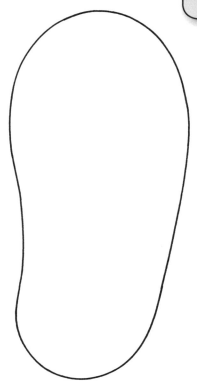

Directions:

1. Have students pair up and trace each other's foot or shoe onto a piece of construction paper, poster board, or cardstock.

2. Each student cuts out his or her footprint and decorates it. Students might draw or write what they can do every day to follow the Lord (smile, be kind, help others, go to Mass, pray).

3. Gather and display the completed footprints in the hallway or around the classroom.

Optional: Older students can compose a prayer to accompany their footprints.

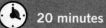
Fish Symbol

Grades 1–4

Materials:

Fish pattern for each student (see page 7)	Glue
Scissors	Sheet of fish scales for each student

FAITH CONNECTION

Explain to the students that the fish was one of the earliest symbols of Jesus because the Greek word for fish, ichthus, *is formed by the first letters of the words* Jesus Christ, Son of God, Savior. *The "scales" represent the people in community with Jesus, forming the Church.*

Directions:

1. Distribute a fish pattern to each student along with a sheet of fish scales representing the people in the Church.

2. Have the students assemble their fishes and glue the pieces of the pattern together. Then have them cut out all the fish scales and glue them onto the fish.

Optional: Some students may want to draw faces on the fish scales.

Fish Symbol Pattern

Our Roots Art Mural

Grades 1–8

Materials:

Roll of white shelf paper or newsprint	Crayons or pain
Brushes	Newspapers

> **FAITH CONNECTION**
>
> *As a good review of salvation history, have the students reflect on the story and heritage of the Church from Abraham and Joseph to the Church in the world today.*

Directions:

1. Have the students put their Church story in art form as a mural.

2. Encourage the students to include themselves as part of the Church in the world today.

Beaded Cross Pins

Grades 3–8

Materials:

Craft stems cut into 2" and 3" lengths	Safety pins, 1 for each child
Pony beads, 12–15 for each child	

1. **2.**

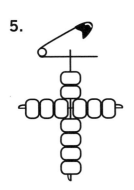

3. & 4.

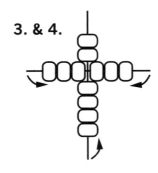

5.

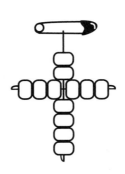

FAITH CONNECTION

Talk about how missionaries carry the Gospel of Jesus to many different lands. Explain that we are all called to share in the mission of the Church, carrying Jesus' message with us wherever we go. Have the children make beaded cross pins to remind them to carry Jesus with them wherever they go.

Directions:

1. Give each child a 2" and a 3" piece of craft stem.

2. Have the child twist the two pieces of craft stem together to form a cross.

3. Thread three pony beads on each "arm" of the cross and then put at least six beads on the central post of the cross.

4. Secure the beads by bending the ends of the craft stem over and around the end beads.

5. Bend the end of craft stem at the top of the cross around the safety pin.

Paper Cranes of Peace

Grades 3–8

Materials:

A square sheet of paper for each child

Directions:

1. Begin with a square sheet of paper.

2. Fold the square in half diagonally, forming a triangle.

3. Fold triangle in half so that corner A meets corner B. Make a hard crease along the fold. You will have two triangles, A and B.

4. Place one hand flat on the B triangle to hold it in place. Place the other hand inside triangle A to open it like a pocket.

5. Fold corner A (the top of the pocket) down to meet corner C (the base of the pocket). Flatten out the pocket to create a diamond shape.

6. Turn the paper over and repeat the pocket fold with triangle B. You should end up with two diamond shapes, one on top of the other.

7. With the open ends pointing toward you, fold the two corners on the top layer in so that the bottom edges are lined up with the center line of the paper. See diagram.

8. Turn the paper over and repeat on the other side. When you're done, you should have a little kite.

9. Fold down the little triangle at the top of the kite, first one way, then the other. Make a hard crease on both sides.

10. Undo the folds made in steps 7, 8, and 9. You should have the folded diamond that you had in step 6, only with creases from steps 7, 8, and 9 visible.

11. Pull up the top layer at point G. Think of it as opening a bird's beak. As you open the beak, fold in sides E and F so that they meet in the middle, with point G at the top. Flatten to a form a long diamond shape. See diagram.

12. Turn the paper over and repeat on the other side. The bottom of the diamond should look like a pair of legs.

FAITH CONNECTION

Explain that, according to Japanese legend, anyone who folds a thousand paper cranes is granted a wish. Since the bombing of Hiroshima in 1945, paper cranes have become an international symbol of the wish for peace. Point out that Jesus told his apostles "I leave you peace, my peace I give you" and that, if we want peace in the world, we must share the peace of Christ with others.

13. Open the side of one of the legs. Bring up point H by folding the leg up and turning the crease inside out. Press the leg flat.

14. Repeat this step with the other side.

15. Crimp one of the points to make the crane's head.

16. Open wings to complete the crane.

17. You can make your crane flap its wings. Hold the lowest two points on the body and gently pull them apart.

1.

2.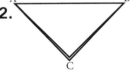

3.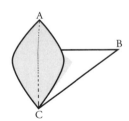

4.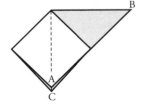

5.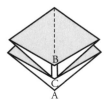

6.

7.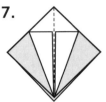

8.

9.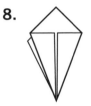

10.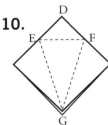

11.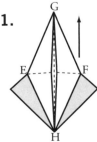

12.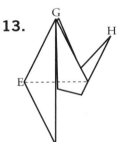

13.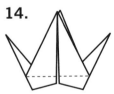

14.

15.

16.

People Collage

Grades 1–8

Materials:

Old magazines	Magic markers
Scissors	Rulers
Glue	Pencils
Colored construction paper	

FAITH CONNECTION

Remind the children that we are the Church —the People of God.

Directions:

1. Cut out the faces of people from old magazines.

2. Glue the faces to a large piece of construction paper.

3. Print "We are the Church" at the top for grades 1 and 2. (Younger children may do the printing themselves if they are able.)

4. Direct older children to arrange the faces in a shape or symbol that represents Church. They may draw their own symbol or drawing of a church first and then arrange the faces inside the symbol. (See sample idea.)

5. Cut out the symbol containing the faces and glue it to a larger piece of construction paper of a contrasting color.

6. Print "We are the Church" on the larger piece of construction paper.

 30 minutes

Jesus' Baptism: A Dove Mobile

Grades 1–4

Materials:

Paper plate, 1 per student	Glue
Pencil	Hole punch
Scissors	Yarn
Packing peanuts or cotton balls	Dove Pattern (see page 14)

> ### FAITH CONNECTION
> *Read the Bible story of Jesus' baptism (Matthew 3:13–17). Point out that the story tells us that Holy Spirit descended on Jesus like a dove and that the dove has come to be seen as a symbol of the Holy Spirit.*

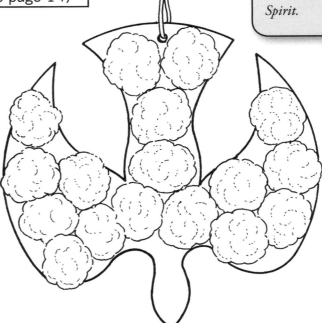

Directions:

1. Following the illustration on page 14 as a guide, use a pencil to draw a dove shape on the paper plate. Cut out the dove shape.

2. Glue packing peanuts or cotton balls over both sides of the dove.

3. Punch a hole in the tail of the dove, tie on a piece of yarn, and hang up your mobile.

4. Thank God for your Baptism.

5. Additional suggestions
   • Use the dove for lessons on Noah's ark or Pentecost.
   • Write your baptismal date on a dove shape. Hang it up in your room as a reminder of the day you became God's child in Baptism.
   • Cover the dove with white yarn or crumpled pieces of white tissue paper.

Dove Pattern

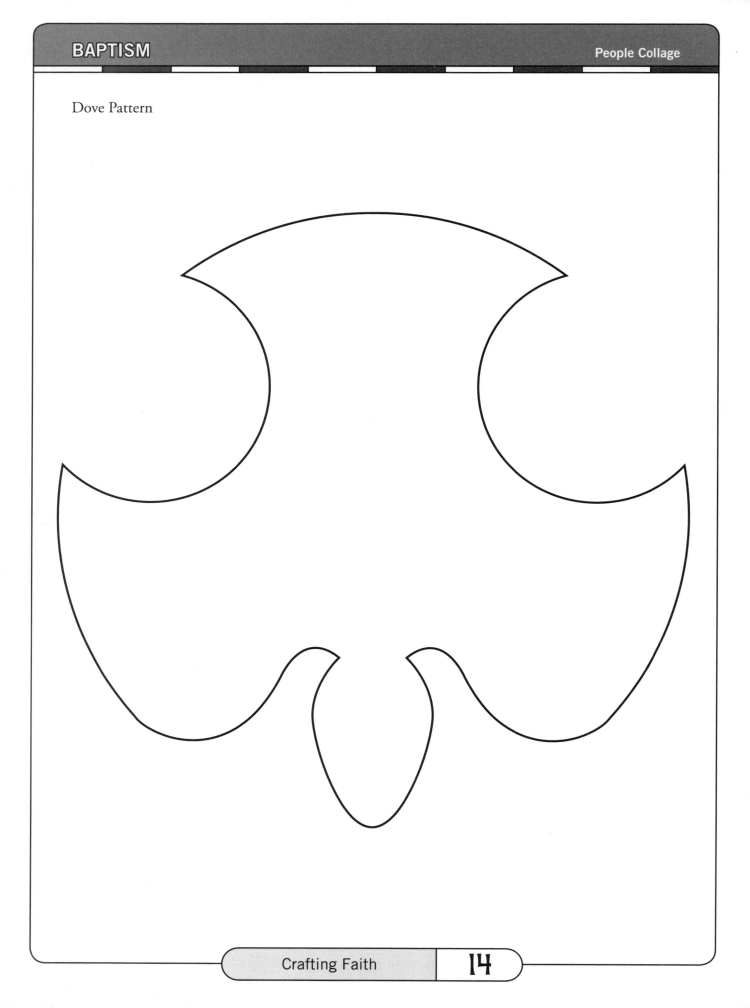

Baptism Mobile

Grades 1–4

Materials:

Cardboard	Glue
Mobile patterns of baptismal symbols (see page 16)	Cellophane tape
Scissors	Coat hanger
Construction paper	Paper punch
Thread or yarn	Pencils

You may need teacher aides for this project.

> **FAITH CONNECTION**
>
> *Ask if any of the children have seen a baptism before and discuss their experiences. Explain that the four symbols of Baptism are water, oil, fire, and a white garment.*

Before Class:

Fold a large piece of blue construction paper in half to make the water symbol that will be used to encase the hanger. At the open end of the construction paper, draw and cut out waves. Glue the water symbol at the top of the waves and around the hanger. Prepare sets of baptismal symbols on cardboard for the students to trace.

Directions:

1. Have the students trace the cardboard symbols onto construction paper.

2. Cut out the symbols.

3. Punch a hole in each symbol.

4. Using tape or glue, attach yarn or thread in different lengths to each symbol.

5. Hang the candle, robe, and oil symbols from the water symbol.

6. Loop a piece of yarn or thread through the top of the water frame for hanging.

7. Tie symbols in various lengths to water symbol (hanger).

Baptism Mobile Patterns
Grades 1–4 and 5–8

 20 minutes

Baptism Mobile

Grades 5–8

Materials:

Mobile patterns of baptismal symbols (see page 16)	Scissors
Cardboard	Paper punch
String or yarn	Colored tissue paper: blue for water, yellow for oil, gold or orange for the candle, white for the garment

FAITH CONNECTION

Ask if any of the children have seen a baptism before and discuss their experiences. Explain that the four symbols of Baptism are water, oil, fire, and a white garment.

Directions:

1. Have the students trace two sets of the symbols for the sacrament of Baptism onto the cardboard.

2. Cut out the patterns for each symbol and prepare to glue them together later.

3. Cut out the center of each of the symbols, leaving an opening in the middle for tissue paper.

4. Use different-colored tissue papers to decorate and accentuate the insides of the symbols.

5. Glue tissue paper to one of the symbols and then place its twin on the top.

6. Reinforce the water symbol on the hanger itself with a strip of cardboard at the bottom. Then hang the other symbols from the water symbol.

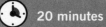

My Birthday as a Christian

Grades 5–8

Materials:

My Birthday as a Christian certificate, 1 for each student (see page 19)	Pens or pencils

(see page 19)

FAITH CONNECTION

Explain to the children that our baptism day can be thought of as our birthday as a Christian since we are "born again" in Jesus.

My Birthday as a Christian

I became a member of my human family on the day of my birth.

I was born on June 24, 2000 .

My family name is Jones .

I became a member of God's family at my Baptism.

The day I was born to new life with Christ was July 30, 2000 .

The name I received at Baptism is Anne .

My godparents are Keith and Suzy Michaels .

The priest or deacon who baptized me was Fr John Smith .

The church where I was baptized was Saint Joan of Arc .

Directions:

1. Distribute copies of the My Birthday as a Christian certificate to all students.

2. Have the students fill in the blanks they can on their own. Have students take the activity home to fill in the remaining blanks with help from their parents or guardians.

3. Have the students share their work during the next class.

My Birthday as a Christian Certificate Pattern

My Birthday as a Christian

❧

I became a member of my human family on the day of my birth.

I was born on _____ .

My family name is _____ .

❧

I became a member of God's family at my Baptism.

The day I was born to new life with Christ was _____ .

The name I received at Baptism is _____ .

My godparents are _____ .

The priest or deacon who baptized me was _____ .

The church where I was baptized was _____ .

 25 minutes

Baptism Candle

Grades 1–4

Materials:

Votive candle or inexpensive white taper for each student	Sequins or glitter
Glue	

> **FAITH CONNECTION**
>
> *Give each of the students one candle. Tell them that this candle represents the baptismal candle which symbolizes the light of Christ.*

Directions:

1. Have the students decorate their candles with different-colored sequins or roll the candles in glitter.

2. When the students take their candles home, the candles will need to be put in candle holders. Suggest that the students use these candles for special family celebrations or light them for prayer at mealtime.

🕐 25 minutes

Painted Seashells

Grades 3–8

Materials:

Clean seashells	Brushes
Tempera paint	Newspapers
Liquid soap	Containers for the paint

FAITH CONNECTION
Point out that it is common for priests and deacons to use a seashell to pour the waters of baptism over the heads of those being baptized.

Directions:

1. Mix a few drops of liquid soap into the tempera paint. The soap will help the paint stick to the shell.

2. Have the students paint their names and dates of Baptism on the outside of the shells.

3. Have the students paint an appropriate scene on the inside of the shells.

Seashell Mosaics

Grades 1–3

Materials:

Small seashells of various sizes	Large mixing spoon
Plaster of paris (available at hardware stores)	Plastic planter saucers
Mixing container	

Directions:

1. Since plaster dries rather quickly, encourage the children to plan out their mosaic by laying the shells onto a hard surface in the designs they desire. Keep designs very simple by providing a limited number of shells to each child.

2. Mix plaster according to the directions on the package.

3. Pour into plastic saucers.

4. Set shells onto the poured plaster.

5. Allow time to dry, usually 30 minutes depending on humidity and temperature.

Note: Work with very small numbers of children at a time since plaster dries quickly and is not as forgiving as other mediums.

 **20 minutes**

Baptism Water Blessing

Grades 1–8

Materials:

Clear bowl	Ribbon
Water	Permanent marker
Seashell	

FAITH CONNECTION
Enhance your baptism lessons or observe the baptism of Jesus in January with the following ideas.

"Happy Baptism Day"

Directions:

1. Plan a Baptism party with cake and balloons for the children in your class. Sing "Happy Baptism Day" to the tune of "Happy Birthday." This activity could be done in January around the time of the Feast of the Baptism of the Lord.

2. Use water to say a special blessing. Put a clear bowl of water in the center of the group. Pass the water around and, one at a time, have the children dip their fingers into the water and touch their foreheads, saying, "God, bless my head"; touch their lips, saying, "God, bless my lips"; and touch their hearts, saying, "God, bless my heart. Amen."

3. Collect a seashell for each child in your group. Tell the children that the seashell is often used as a symbol of the water used in Baptism. Print each child's name on a shell as a reminder of his or her Baptism. If possible drill a hole in each shell and lace a ribbon through the hole for hanging. Add a small piece of paper to the ribbon with the blessing "May God bless you and keep you always" or "You are God's child."

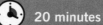

Baptism Book

Grades 1–5

Materials:

Two sheets of construction paper per child	Aluminum foil
Pictures of children's Baptism	Candle
Markers	White ribbon or fabric

Directions:

1. Use two sheets of construction paper folded together in half to create the following pages as you discuss Baptism.

   Cover—A photo of each child's Baptism. Discuss why families decide to have their children baptized.

   Page 1—Have the children cut drops from the aluminum foil to symbolize water. Encourage them to make a pattern as they paste them on the page. Discuss all of the wonderful things water does for us such as cooling, cleaning, and refreshing us. Explain that God provides us all of these and even more.

   Page 2—Carefully light a candle away from the children. Allowing the children to watch, place a few drops of candle wax on the page. Remind them that lighting a candle must be done by an adult because the flame of a candle can burn a person. Wait until the wax has completely dried and then let the children gently touch it.
   Explain that parents and godparents are asked to hold a candle during the Baptism ceremony to remind them of the light God brings into their lives.

   Page 3—Have the children draw several smiling faces. Tell the children that the community gathers together to pray for support and to welcome the newest members.

   Page 4—Have the children draw an open Bible or glue individual words cut from a newspaper. Show the children a Bible. Tell them that we share God's Word when we celebrate Baptism.

   Page 5—Attach a piece of white fabric. Tell the children that a white garment is worn to remind us that we are God's children.

2. When the books are complete, invite the children to take the books home and share what they have learned with their families.

> **FAITH CONNECTION**
> *Children become familiar with many of the symbols of Baptism through everyday living. Make Baptism books to help them make important connections between their experiences and a beginning understanding of these symbols of the sacrament.*

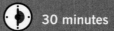

Fruits of the Holy Spirit Box

Grades 6–8

Materials:

Box with a lid, 1 per student	Newspapers
Magazine pictures and/or magazines	Paint brushes
Art supplies (crayons, magic markers, watercolor paints)	Scissors
Glue	

Before Class:

Unless the boxes are new, you may wish to paint the boxes and lids inside and outside with white latex paint.

Directions:

1. Give each student a box with a lid.

2. List the Fruits of the Holy Spirit on the board:

Charity	**Generosity**
Joy	**Gentleness**
Peace	**Faithfulness**
Patience	**Modesty**
Kindness	**Self-control**
Goodness	**Chastity**

3. Using magazine pictures, have the students glue pictures onto the box that reveal the students' own Fruits of the Holy Spirit.

4. Students may use quotes from poems, prayers, advertisements, or their own words to caption their creations. Allow options and exploration.

 20 minutes

Pinwheels

Grades 1–4

Materials:

Colored construction paper (7½" square)	Stapler or glue
Pinwheel pattern (see page 29)	Pencils
Plastic straws	Scissors
Hole punch	Paper fasteners or pins

> **FAITH CONNECTION**
>
> *The wind is an idea that can help us understand the presence of the Holy Spirit. The Bible speaks of the Holy Spirit in symbols of fire and wind. The wind cannot be seen and yet the effect of the wind is very real to us. The Holy Spirit is God's presence with us. As the students make the pinwheels and watch them turn in the wind, remind the students that the Holy Spirit is moving in their hearts.*

Directions:

1. Trace the pinwheel pattern on a square piece of colored construction paper. Then cut it out. Gently fold up each section from the tip to the center and staple or glue all four at the center.

2. Punch a hole through the center of the pinwheel and through the top of the straw in order to insert a paper fastener through both items. Spread the paper fastener's prongs on the back side of the straw to secure it in place. Pins may be substituted for fasteners.

Pinwheel Pattern

🕐 25 minutes

Holy Spirit Paper Mobile

Grades 1–8

Materials:

Cardboard pattern of Holy Spirit mobile pieces (see page 31)	Scissors
White poster board	Pencils
Red construction paper	Paper punch
White yarn or string	Stapler or cellophane tape
Small plastic ring (optional)	

With younger students, you may need teacher aides for this project.

FAITH CONNECTION

Review with the children two symbols of the Holy Spirit that come to us from Scripture: a dove (Matthew 3:16) and tongues of fire (Acts of the Apostles 2:3).

Before Class:

Prepare adequate numbers of cardboard patterns for the Holy Spirit mobile. For younger students, you may wish to precut the dove symbol out of the white poster board. Mark with a small "x" where the student should punch out the holes. Then proceed to step 3 during class.

Directions:

1. Trace the dove pattern on white poster board. Mark with an "x" where the holes should go.

2. Cut out the dove and punch out the holes.

3. Trace seven "tongues of fire" or flames (see page 31 for a pattern) on the red construction paper and cut them out.

4. Tie various lengths (6"–12" long) of yarn to the Holy Spirit dove symbol.

5. Staple or tape one flame to each piece of yarn.

6. Tie one 8" length of yarn to the top of the dove. Make a loop and tie it into a knot. You might want to tie a small plastic ring to the top in order to hang up the mobile.

Optional: Have the students write a gift of the Holy Spirit (Wisdom, Understanding, Knowledge, Counsel, Fortitude, Piety, Fear of the Lord) on each flame.

Holy Spirit Paper Mobile Pattern
Grades 1–8

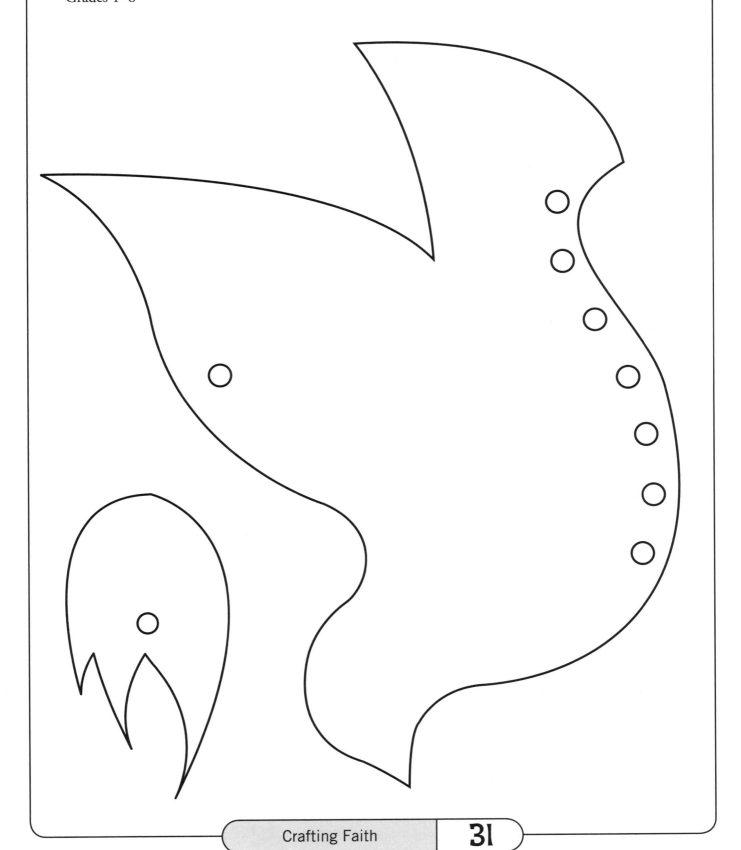

25 minutes

Holy Spirit Felt Mobile

Grades 5–8

Materials:

Cardboard pattern of Holy Spirit pieces, 1 per student	White glue
Scissors	Pencils
White felt	Small plastic ring— one per student
Red felt	Paper punch
White yarn or string	

FAITH CONNECTION
Review with the children two symbols of the Holy Spirit that come to us from Scripture: a dove (Matthew 3:16) and tongues of fire (Acts of the Apostles 2:3).

Before Class:

Prepare cardboard patterns of dove and "tongues of fire" (flame). Make a sample mobile.

Directions:

1. Using the cardboard patterns, trace two doves on the white felt.
2. Cut out and glue the two felt doves onto the cardboard dove—one on each side. (With cardboard "sandwiched" in the middle, the dove is made more durable.)
3. Set the dove aside to dry.
4. Trace the "tongues of fire" (flame) pattern on the red felt seven times.
5. Cut out and punch a hole near the top of each flame.
6. Punch seven holes along the bottom of the dove and one hole on top for hanging. (See pattern for placement of holes.)
7. Tie one piece of yarn approximately 7" long to the top of the dove. Tie the other end of the yarn to the plastic ring for hanging.
8. Using different lengths of white yarn, tie and hang the flames from the dove so that the mobile is balanced.

Name Plaque

Grades 5–8

Materials:

5½" x 8½" piece of white paper for each student	White Glue
Poster board	*What's in a Name?* book or another book with meanings of names
Permanent markers with fine points and wide points	Book of saints
Pencils	Bible
Rulers	

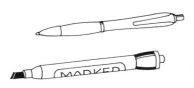

Before Class:

Look up each student's name. Prepare the meaning of each name or the characteristic you have observed. Type, write, or print an appropriate Bible verse on a white piece of paper. This will be glued to the bottom section of the plaque.

Directions:

1. Cover the table and floor with newspaper.

2. Have the students practice designing their own first names on scrap paper.

3. Draw parallel lines (1" to 1½" apart) lightly in pencil on the piece of white paper for the name. ½" below the name put the meaning of the name (½" high). Leave a space of ½" between the name and its meaning. Arrange the meaning of name or characteristic in a ½" space.

4. Lightly pencil in name in the top 1" to 1½" space. Try to center it, allowing space for wide marker.

5. Skip the next ½" space.

FAITH CONNECTION

God calls us each by name. This project affirms the student's identity as a child of God who has been called by name as very special and precious to God.

*The resource book **What's in a Name?** by Linda Frances, John Hartzell, and Al Palmquist (ARK Products, Minneapolis, Minn., 1976) contains over seven hundred names and their meanings. It gives the literal meaning of a name and a suggested character quality with an appropriate scripture verse. This approach is different from that of secular name books.*

Some names may be difficult to find. You may have to use other name books to find the meaning of a name or you can give students a positive characteristic that you have observed in them, such as faithfulness, a gentle spirit, or truthfulness. Give each student a special Bible verse that will strengthen the student.

This is a two-part project. Students prepare names in one session and finish the plaque in the next session.

6. Using pencil, lightly write a characteristic or meaning of the student's name in the ½" space. Center carefully. You will use the fine-point marker for this part.

7. Trace over the pencil lines with markers. Use wide markers for the name. Use fine point markers for characteristic of the name.

8. Glue white paper with the name on it to the poster board to form the plaque.

9. Glue an appropriate Scripture verse to the bottom of the plaque.

WAYNE
LIFTER of CARES

"Bear one another's burdens, and so you will fulfill the law of Christ."

–Galations 6:2

Handprints

Grades 1–4

Materials:

5½" x 8½" piece of white paper, poster board, or felt for each student	Markers or other materials for decorating
Pencils or pens	Scissors

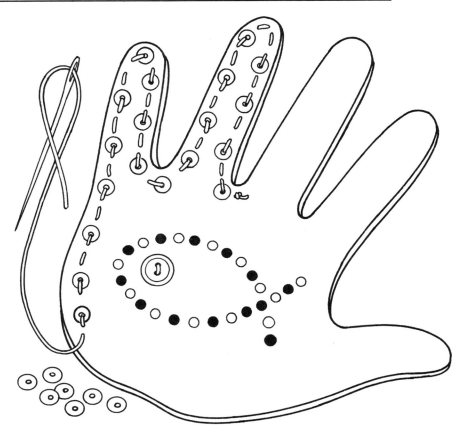

FAITH CONNECTION

When we come together to celebrate the liturgy, we share the Body of Christ with one another. It is important that we share with others so that we are generous and loving people who are concerned about other people. The Handprints that we will be making can show how, strengthened by the Eucharist, we can reach out to other people.

Directions:

1. Give each student a piece of paper, poster board, or felt.

2. Have the students trace both of their hands on the piece of paper, poster board, or felt.

3. Cut out the handprints.

4. Decorate the handprints, using markers or other materials. Students may write their favorite Bible verses or prayers on their handprints.

5. Encourage the students to reach out to other people and give their handprints to two people they select.

Storyblock

Grades 1–4

Materials:

Poster board	Scissors
Block pattern (see page 37)	Crayons or drawing pencils
White glue	

FAITH CONNECTION

At the Last Supper, Jesus gave us the gift of the Eucharist. Strengthened by the Body and Blood of Jesus, we seek ways to nourish others physically and spiritually.

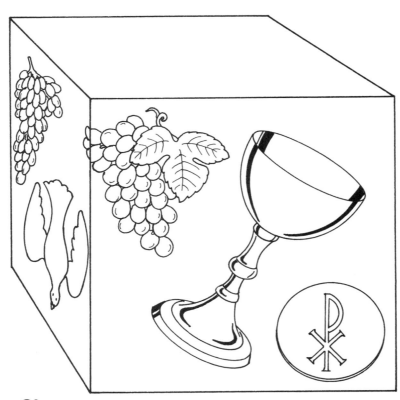

Before Class:

Make ample block patterns for your class to use.

Directions:

1. Make a pattern for a block that resembles the one in the sketch. Dimensions may vary as long as the sections are square.

2. Trace the pattern twice on the poster board. Cut out the two pieces.

3. Fold up the outside sections of each piece. Glue one half of the block inside the other half of the block.

4. Decorate each side of the block with pictures that symbolize the Eucharist, the Last Supper, or ways people nourish each other spiritually and/or physically.

Storyblock Pattern

Eucharist Symbols

Laced Picture Plaque

Grades 1–4

Materials:

Paper plates, 2 per student	Artificial flowers or natural materials such as acorn caps, unusual small stones, and seeds
Construction paper	Crayons
Yarn	Pencils
Paper punch	Scissors
White glue	

You may need aides for this project.

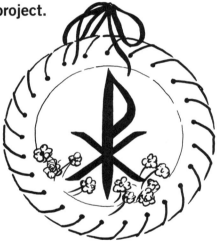

Before Class:

Punch holes equidistant around the outside of the paper plate about one-fourth inch from the edge.

Directions:

1. On the construction paper, have the students color symbols of the Eucharist. You may provide symbols to trace, or the students may draw their own. Examples: bread and wine, a Chi-Rho (pictured), a host and a chalice, and the Last Supper.

2. After the students have colored their symbols, the symbols should be cut out.

3. Glue the Eucharist symbol in the center of the plate. Glue artificial flowers or other materials onto the plate to decorate around the Eucharist symbol.

4. Lace yarn through the holes around the plate. (Allow enough lacing at the beginning and the end to tie for hanging.)

Symbols of Faith Magnets

Grades 1–8

Materials:

Felt or poster board	White glue
Scissors	Magnet strips
Crayons, colored pencils, or markers	

Directions:

1. Give each student a piece of felt or poster board.

2. Have the students draw a miniature loaf of bread, one slice of bread, or a biscuit.

3. Cut out the bread symbols that the students have drawn.

4. Decorate the symbols using crayons, colored pencils, or markers. Students may want to draw a cross symbol on their bread creations.

5. Using white glue, attach a magnetic strip to the back of the bread symbols. You may wish to attach a scripture verse to each.

6. Have the students take the magnets home and place them on their refrigerators. Students could make extras for gifts.

Optional: Students may draw other Christian symbols (Chi-Rho, cross, dove, etc.).

Handprint Cloth for First Eucharist Celebration

Grades 2–4

Materials:

1 or more king-size sheets (of a size suitable for the altar)	Flat foil pans and foam paint rollers
Several colors of fabric paint or fabric pen markers	Water and paper towels for cleanup

> **FAITH CONNECTION**
> *In this project, children (with the help of parents or other adults) prepare a cloth for the altar with their handprints and names for First Eucharist*

Directions:

1. Prepare—or have a volunteer prepare—a cloth suitable to be used on the altar for First Eucharist. It may be necessary to sew several sheets together.

2. Decide on a symbol or emblem, such as a chalice, for the center of the cloth and then mask off the area.

3. On the day of the activity, arrange an area where the cloth can be laid out. Put small quantities of the various colored paints in separate pans.

4. Have each child come up individually to choose a color. Instruct the child to put his or her hands in the paint, palms down and flat. Then use foam paint rollers to spread the paint evenly over the child's hands. Immediately transfer the child's hands to the cloth and press them down for 2 to 3 minutes. Print or write the child's name close to his or her handprints.

5. After the paint is dry, paint the symbol on the center of the cloth. If you want, add a ribbon trim to decorate the cloth.

Coloring with Yarn Cross

Grades 1–4

Materials:

Poster board (approximately 5" × 8"), 1 per student	White glue
Colored yarn	Paper punch
Scissors	Ruler
Newspaper	

FAITH CONNECTION

Jesus died on the cross to forgive our sins. In the Sacrament of Reconciliation, we celebrate this forgiveness.

Before Class:

Cut the poster board. Cut yarn into 12" lengths for grades 1 and 2.
Punch holes in the top of the cross and add yarn in order to hang the cross.

Directions:

1. Have the students draw a large, simple cross on the poster board. (Check to see that it is large enough.) The students may use a ruler if they wish.

2. Cut a piece of yarn about 12" in length.

3. Spread glue on the vertical bar of the cross.

4. Starting at the outside edge of the cross, press the yarn gently to the poster board, spiraling inward. Trim excess yarn or add more until all the cross area is filled in.

5. Fill in the horizontal bar of the cross in the same manner. You may do the two sides separately or glue yarn right over the vertical bar.

6. To hang, punch two holes near the top of the poster board and string a piece of yarn through them. Make a knot behind each hole to secure the yarn.

Coloring with
Yarn Cross Pattern

Works of Mercy Tree

Grades 1–4

Materials:

Coffee can	Leafless tree branch
Gift wrapping paper	Yarn
Glue	Paper punch
Plaster of paris	

You may need one or two aides for this project.

> **FAITH CONNECTION**
> *Explain that the Corporal and Spiritual Works of Mercy are concrete ways of showing our love of neighbors.*

Directions:

1. Cover a coffee can with gift wrapping paper.

2. Fill the coffee can with plaster of paris. Set the branch down into the plaster of paris and hold the branch upright.

3. Have the students make little booklets from gift wrapping paper and write a promise to perform a work of mercy inside each booklet. (One or two aides will be needed to help the younger students write their works.)

4. Write the Corporal and Spiritual Works of Mercy on the board.

Corporal Works of Mercy	Spiritual Works of Mercy
Feeding the hungry	Instructing
Sheltering the homeless	Advising
Clothing the naked	Consoling
Visiting the sick and those in prison	Comforting
Giving alms to the poor	Forgiving
Burying the dead	Bearing wrongs with patience

5. Punch a hole in each booklet. Using yarn, tie each booklet to the tree.

6. Help the students remember to do their works of mercy by suggesting they make a "promise" tree at home.

7. This project can be brought to the liturgy and presented as the students' gift.

The Old Rugged Cross

Grades 1–8

Materials:

Twigs, 2 per student	Wire or masking tape
Brown yarn	

FAITH CONNECTION

Explain to the children that there is a traditional Christian hymn named "The Old Rugged Cross" and that today they will be designing one.

Directions:

1. Wire or tape two twigs together to form a cross.

2. Wrap twigs completely with brown yarn.

More Ideas for Crosses:

Fabric cross: Cut a scrap of fabric material into the shape of a cross. Glue the cross to a piece of poster board, burlap, or felt. (Grades 1–2)

Wallpaper cross: Use old wallpaper sample books. Pick out a wallpaper design. (Small prints look fine.) Cut the wallpaper into the shape of a cross. Glue the cross to burlap, felt, or poster board. (Grades 1–2)

A Bible verse could be added to any of the crosses by gluing it to the bottom or top of the cross.

🕐 **20 minutes**

Forgiveness Chain

Grades 1–4

Materials:

Strips of paper, 10 to 20 per student	Pens, pencils, or crayons
Tape	

> **FAITH CONNECTION**
>
> *It is often difficult for children to ask forgiveness of others in their lives or to grant forgiveness to someone who has hurt them because they don't know what words to listen for or to say.*

Directions:

1. Discuss with the children what words they can use to ask or give forgiveness. Phrases like the following can be useful to children.

   I'm sorry.

   Please forgive me.

   I forgive you.

   Peace be with you.

   You're forgiven.

   I was wrong.

2. To help the children remember these words and phrases, show them how to make forgiveness chains. Have the children write a forgiveness phrase on individual paper strips and decorate the strips. Repeat the process with other phrases and strips. Then have the children tape their links together.

3. The completed chain is a reminder that we are to ask forgiveness of people we have injured by our words or our actions. We must also forgive those who have hurt us. Link all the forgiveness chains together for display in the classroom.

 25 minutes

Church Windows

Grades 5–8

Materials:

Sponges	White poster board (any size)
Tempera paint (yellow-green and blue-green)	White glue
Black paper	Black felt-tip pen
White paper	Church windows pattern (see page 49)

FAITH CONNECTION

Tell the children that church windows often contain images that teach us about our faith. Explain that for today's project, they will be creating a church window that teaches.

He was lost
and has been found."
– Luke 15:3

Directions:

1. Dip the sponge into bright yellow-green tempera paint and pat all over the white poster board. Repeat with a deeper blue-green paint, shading heavier in the center.

2. Cut two identical church window frames from the pattern provided, one black and one white. Use glue to fasten the frames over the shaded background.

3. Have the students find Scripture readings taught in the Scripture class. Using felt-tip pens, print a passage on the bottom of the picture.

Note: Leave a space at the bottom of the poster board for printing a Scripture passage.

Church Windows Pattern

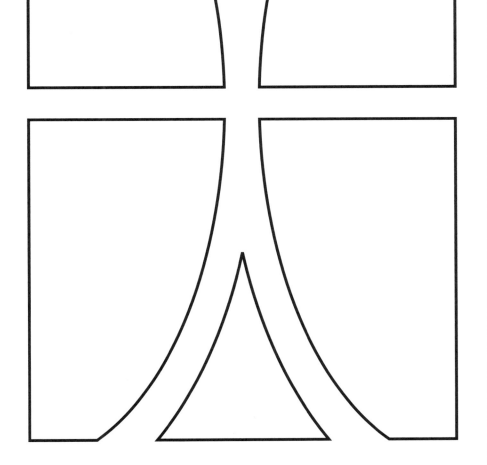

25 minutes

Gift Booklets

Grades 1–4

Materials:

Construction paper	Felt-tip pens
Flower seals or pictures from magazines	Scripture verses, jokes, inspirational poems cut from magazines
Yarn	Glue
Scissors	

Blessed are the clean of heart, for they shall see God.

–Matthew 5:8

Before Class:

1. Cut construction paper into sections of 9" × 6". Use two sections folded in half for each booklet.

2. With a paper punch, punch holes near the fold.

Directions:

1. Pull yarn through the punched holes and tie the yarn in a bow on the outside fold of the booklet.

2. Paste a flower picture on the cover and then alternate pasting flowers and Scripture verses on each of the inside pages to make a Scripture booklet.

3. For a joke booklet, paste a cartoon or several printed jokes on each page. Decorate the remainder of each page with smiling faces drawn with felt-tip pens.

Hug from Me to You

Grades 1–4

Materials:

Paper plates	Construction paper
3" × 12" strips of poster board	Glue
Yarn	Masking tape
Markers	Paper clips

> ### FAITH CONNECTION
> *Greet one another with a holy "hug"—adapted from Romans 16:16*
>
> *Saint Paul urged Christians to greet one another with a holy kiss or embrace. A hug is an embrace. Use these hugs to send a holy embrace to shut-ins or anyone needing some heart warming.*

Directions:

1. Draw facial features on the paper plate, using the markers.

2. Glue on yarn for hair.

3. Cover the poster board with decorative contact paper or fabric and glue in place.

4. Make a collar cut from fabric or construction paper.

5. Trace each child's hands and cut them out to be attached to each end of the covered poster board.

6. Open paper clips and tape them to the back of each hand for easy hanging.

7. Write across the arm span "A hug from me to you!"

Scripture Passage Pencil Holder

Grades 1–4

Materials:

Glass jar or coffee can, 1 per student	Construction paper
Photograph of each child	Pens or pencils
Clear contact paper	

Directions:

1. Make a pen/pencil holder from a jar or coffee can.

2. Take a photo of each child and print it or have the children bring photos of themselves to class.

3. Have children make a new label for the can or jar, using construction paper.

4. Glue or tape each child's photo to his or her label.

5. Have the children write passages from Scripture on the labels.

6. Secure the labels to the can or jar with clear contact paper.

New Year Crackers

Grades 1–8

Materials:

Psalm quotes	Cardboard tube (such as a toilet paper tube)
Crayons or markers	Tissue paper
Candy	Tape, twist ties, or ribbon

> **FAITH CONNECTION**
>
> *Show the children how to make the New Year crackers as gifts for people who are sick.*

Directions:

1. Distribute copies of the following quotations from Psalms.

   Gracious is the LORD and just; yes, our God is merciful (Psalm 116:5).

   May your kindness, O LORD, be upon us; we have put our hope in you (Psalm 33:22).

2. Have the children color and decorate the Scripture verse message.

3. Tell them to put the message and a few candy treats into the cardboard tube.

4. Help the children wrap the filled cardboard tubes with the tissue paper, securing the tissue paper at the ends with tape, twist ties, or ribbon.

5. Allow each child to have one treat.

6. Stickers can be added to the wrapped tubes as decoration.

7. When the children finish, have them bring their gifts to the prayer center.

 25 minutes

Marriage Rings Collage

Grades 1–4

Materials:

Cardboard, approximately 8" square, 2 per student	Old magazines
Pencils	Scissors
Glue or paste	Cellophane tape
Ring pattern (see page 55)	

You may need aides for the younger students.

Before Class:

Cut out an ample supply of ring patterns for your class. For the younger students, you may want to trace the pattern on the cardboard and cut it out.

Directions:

1. Trace the ring pattern twice on the cardboard pieces. Cut out the two rings.

2. Using the magazines, cut out pictures that show various aspects of marriage. You might find some of the following: a young couple at a movie or picnic, a wedding ceremony, a couple eating dinner, a couple at their child's baptism, or an older couple walking together.

3. Cover a work surface with newspaper to keep it clean. Have students glue the pictures in a collage onto the two rings. Let the ring collages dry.

4. Cut one of the rings and link it with the other, taping it back together again afterward.

Marriage Rings Collage Pattern
Grades 1–4 and 5–8

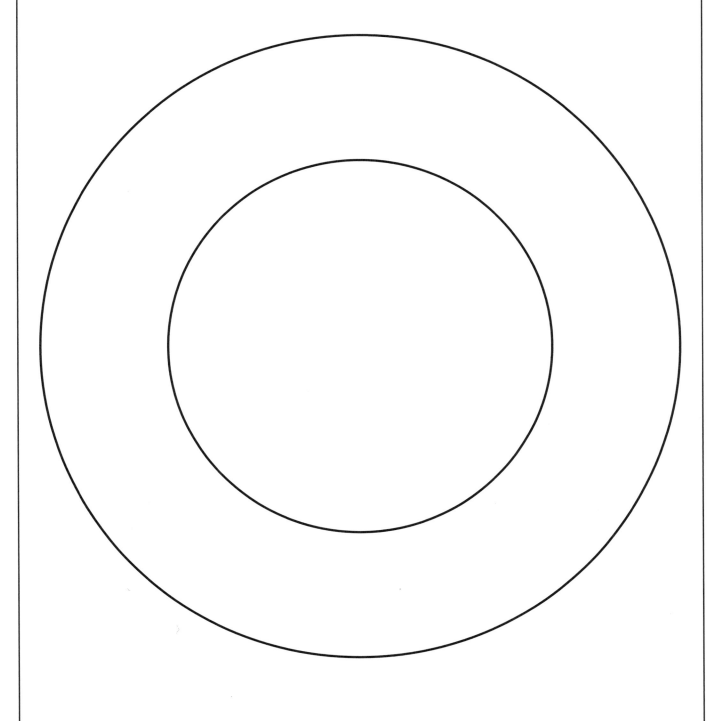

Marriage Rings Collage

Grades 5–8

Materials:

Cardboard, approximately 8" square, 2 per student	Old magazines
Pencils	Scissors
Glue or paste	Newspapers
Cellophane tape	Gold foil or yellow construction paper
Ring pattern (see page 55)	

> **FAITH CONNECTION**
> *In the Rite of Marriage, a man and woman exchange rings as a sign of their unending love for each other.*

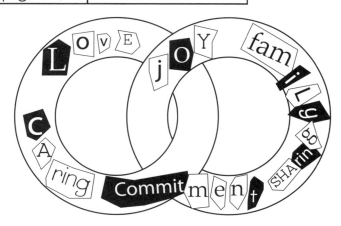

Before Class:

Cut out an ample supply of patterns for your class.

Directions:

1. Trace the ring pattern twice on the cardboard pieces. Cut out the two rings.

2. Trace the ring pattern twice on the gold foil or yellow construction paper. Cut out the two rings.

3. Glue the foil or construction rings onto the cardboard rings.

4. Using the magazines and newspapers, cut out letters and make words that describe various elements of marriage. (The letters that make up the words should be of various colors, sizes, and print styles.)

5. Glue the letters onto the rings. Some words you might end up with are *love, commitment, joy, sharing,* and *caring.*

6. Cut one of the rings and intertwine it with the other, taping it back together again afterward.

Priesthood Mural

Grades 1–8

Materials:

Roll of white shelf paper or newsprint	Newspapers
Crayons, markers, or paints	Paintbrushes

Directions:

1. If using paints, cover a work surface with newspapers.

2. Have the students draw scenes that reflect the ministries of a priest. Some areas to cover are administering the sacraments, ministering to the elderly, visiting the sick, leading others in prayer, preaching homilies, and teaching.

Mural

Grades 1–8

Materials:

Roll of white shelf paper or newsprint	Paint or magic markers
Crayons	

Directions:

1. Brainstorm a list of the signs and symbols of the seven sacraments.

2. Have the students draw symbols of the sacraments and/or sacramentals.

3. Hang the mural on the wall or hang it at a liturgical celebration on the last day of class

Storm and Calm Sea Picture

Grades 1–4

Materials:

Construction paper—light blue, medium blue, black, white, and yellow	Glue
Ruler	Pencils
Picture patterns (see page 60)	Scissors

Directions:

1. Trace and cut out the sections for the picture from construction paper, using the water, lightning, boat, cloud, and sun patterns, Use light blue paper for water, white paper for the white cloud and boat, yellow paper for the sun and lightning, and black paper for the black cloud.

2. For the background, take a full sheet of medium blue construction paper. Make a 3½" fold down from one of the narrow sides.

3. Glue the boat on the water at the bottom of the dark blue folded paper.

4. Beneath the flap, glue the black cloud and lightning. Fold down the top flap and glue the white cloud and sun in place on the top flap.

5. Use the picture to retell the story about faith found in Matthew 8:23–27.

Storm and Calm Sea Picture Patterns

Calm/Stormy Sea Picture

Grades 1–4

Materials:

White paper	Crayons or markers
Light blue construction paper	Scissors
Paper fastener	Pencils

> **FAITH CONNECTION**
> *Begin this project by reading the story of Jesus calming the storm from Matthew 8:23–27 or by telling the story in your own words, stressing Jesus' teaching on faith.*

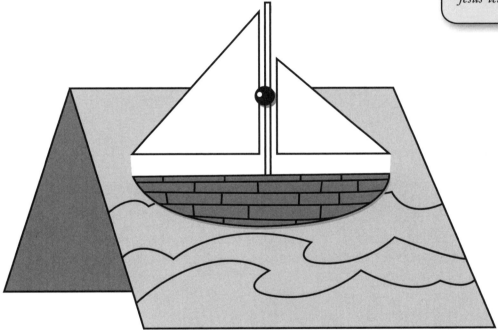

Directions:

1. Have the students cut out a picture of a boat from the white paper.

2. Give each student a piece of blue construction paper with a line drawn across the center. Have the students draw a calm lake on the top half of the paper.

3. Have the students turn the paper upside down and draw a stormy lake on the bottom half of the paper.

4. Have the students color the drawings of the lakes and the boat.

5. With a paper fastener, fasten the boat to the background on the line drawn through the center of the paper. The background can be moved so that the boat will have first a stormy background and then a calm background.

From a Little Seed: A Mosaic Plaque

Grades 1–4

FAITH CONNECTION
Introduce the children to the parable of the mustard seed in Mark 4:30–32.

Materials:

Paper plate	Glue
Markers or crayons	Hole punch
Dried split peas	Yarn

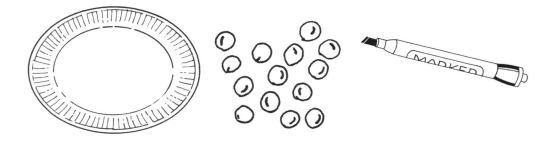

Directions:

1. Write "The Mustard Seed" around the bottom rim of the paper plate.

2. Draw birds around the rest of the rim.

3. In the top center of the plate, draw a circle to represent a treetop. Draw a horizontal line to represent the ground across the bottom third of the plate. Draw a vertical line from the circle to the ground to serve as a tree trunk.

4. Glue a single split pea at the bottom of the vertical line.

5. Glue dried split peas inside the circle to fill in the tree.

6. Punch a hole at the top of the plate, tie yarn through it, and hang it up as a reminder of how God's kingdom grows like a big plant from a tiny seed.

Suggestions:

1. Glue a real mustard seed at the base of the tree trunk.

2. Outline the treetop, trunk, and ground with yarn.

3. Cut little pieces of feathers and glue them to the drawings of birds.

4. Omit the split peas and fill in the tree with green yarn, torn pieces of paper, or wadded pieces of tissue.

5. Color the picture with crayons or markers.

6. Use brown beans to outline the tree trunk.

Sea Painting

Grades 1–8

Materials:

12" × 18" white paper	Blue and black tempera paint
Small sponge	Water
Paintbrush	Newspapers

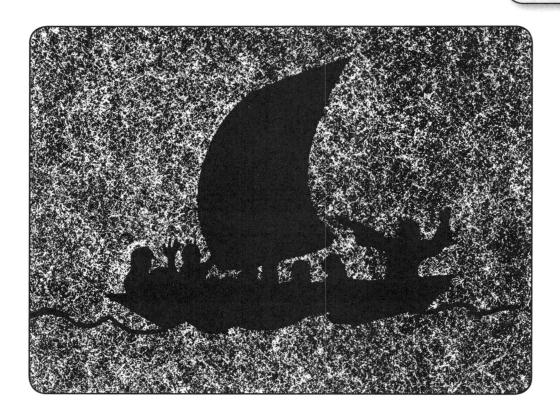

Directions:

1. Cover a work surface with newspapers.

2. Wet the sponge and sponge-paint the background blue by dabbing, blotting, or rubbing the blue paint on white paper. Allow to dry briefly.

3. Use the black paint to paint a boat and voyagers, showing Jesus calming the stormy sea.

Creation Place Mats

Grades 1–4

Materials:

Construction paper or 9" × 12" poster board	"Found" materials from God's creation—dried leaves, dried flowers, weeds, seeds, etc.
Glue or paste	Crayons or felt-tip pens
Clear contact paper	Optional: magazines, scissors

FAITH CONNECTION

Read the first Creation story in Genesis 1–2:3 or summarize it in your own words.

You may wish to have the students write the words Thank You, God *at the top of their place mats. Discuss with the students how thankful we should be for all the things God created. When the place mats are used, they can be prayer starters to thank God for food and for all of creation.*

Directions:

1. Arrange "found" materials on the paper. Glue or paste in place.

2. Have each student design his or her name on the place mat, using the crayons or pens.

3. Let the students continue to decorate or design their place mats, using their own imaginations.

4. Seal the finished creation place mats between two pieces of clear contact paper.

Optional: Have the students cut out magazine pictures that show creation (trees, flowers, animals, etc.) and use those pictures to decorate their place mats.

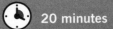 20 minutes

Natural Necklace

Grades 1–5

Materials:

| Yarn | Pinecones or other natural materials |

FAITH CONNECTION

Remind the children that all of creation reflects the glory of God. Invite them to make a necklace of natural items found in God's creation.

Directions:

1. Wind yarn around a pinecone or other natural material to make a necklace.

2. Make one to keep and one to give away.

God's Helpful Creatures: A Ladybug and a Daddy Longlegs

Grades 3–8

FAITH CONNECTION

Begin this project by reading the story of Creation from Genesis 1 or by telling the story in your own words.

Remind the children that God created all living creatures and that all of creation reflects God's presence and glory.

Materials:

Black and white construction paper	Black, white, and orange crayons or markers
Paper plate	Scissors
Glue	Yarn

Directions:

1. Decide which animal you want to make.

2. To make the ladybug, color an orange background and black spots onto the back of a paper plate. Cut a head out of black construction paper and use a white crayon to draw spots for eyes. Cut six short black strips of construction paper for legs; fold each strip down once for a "knee" and up once for a "foot." Cut two thin strips of paper for antennae. Glue the head, legs, and antennae onto the paper plate.

3. To make the daddy longlegs spider, color the back side of a paper plate gray or brown. Cut eight long, black strips of construction paper, accordion-fold them, and glue them around the paper plate for legs. Cut two white ovals for eyes and draw a black spot in each one. Fold each oval down on one end, and glue them onto the back side of the plate.

4. Use a pen to punch a hole in the middle of the ladybug or spider. Tie a loop of yarn through the hole and hang up your creepy-crawly creature.

5. Talk about how God made ladybugs and daddy longlegs to help us.

Suggestions:

1. Use black yarn for the legs and/or antennae.

2. Cut spots out of construction paper to glue onto the ladybug.

Acrostic Prayer

Grades 1–8

Materials:

White construction paper, 1 per student	Crayons or markers
Pencils	

Directions:

1. Have each student print the letters of his or her name vertically on the paper.

2. Have the students think of things in this world for which they would like to thank God. Have the students choose things that begin with each letter in their names. The students should print these things horizontally on their paper, using a letter from their name as the first letter in each word.

3. Have the students embellish their acrostic prayer by illustrating the things for which they are thankful.

Note: You may need aides to help the younger students with the printing.

Gifts of God

Grades 1–8

Materials:

Paper boxes, 1 for each child	Magazine pictures
Light-colored wrapping paper	Ribbon

FAITH CONNECTION

Wrap up a box and use it to illustrate the many gifts of God.

Remind the children that creation is a gift from God and that it is good for us to give thanks for this gift.

Directions:

1. Wrap the box in wrapping paper and tie with a bow.

2. Glue magazine pictures or draw pictures of the gifts of God onto the package.

3. Add a gift tag that says "The Gifts of God."

Art Mural

Grades 1–8

Materials:

Shelf paper or newsprint	Tempera paint or water colors
Paintbrushes	

Directions:

1. Place the paper either on the floor or attach it to a wall.

2. Have the students illustrate God's love and activity in their lives using tempera paint or water colors.

3. Allow the students to work in groups on a particular scene.

4. Display the mural scenes along the wall.

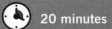 20 minutes

Calendar of God's Love

Grades 1–8

Materials:

Sheets of paper (8½" x 11")	Crayons, pencils, or felt-tip markers
Ruler	

FAITH CONNECTION

Talk to the children about how God loves and cares for us each and every day of our lives.

SUN.	MON.	TUES.	WED.	THUR.	FRI.	SAT.
Prayer	Smile	Helping hands	Act of ♡ Love			

Directions:

1. On a sheet of paper, have the children make a calendar for themselves using a pencil and ruler. The calendar may show only a month or the whole summer vacation. For longer calendars, you may need to provide additional paper.

2. Each child may write what he or she will do every day to help others know God's love and care.

3. Tell the children they may write prayers, actions, or words that tell about God.

Jesus and Me

Grades 1–4

Materials:

One square (6½" × 6½") of poster board per student	One small square photograph of each student (approximately 1½")
Felt-tip markers	White glue
Yarn or string	Paper punch

FAITH CONNECTION

The apostles were chosen by Jesus to be his friends and to witness to others. God chooses each Christian to do the same in today's world. In this activity, students will make a special plaque to hang in their rooms to remind them that Jesus loves them. Just as our photograph reflects what we look like, Jesus calls us to reflect his love to others.

Before Class:

Pencil in the letters of the words *Jesus Loves Me* (1" block printing) around the edges of the poster board. (See drawing for placement of words.) You may wish to prepunch two holes near the top and add the yarn or string for hanging before giving the poster board pieces to the students.

Directions:

1. Have the students trace over the letters with felt-tip pens.

2. Glue the photograph in the center. Let dry.

3. Punch two holes near the top of the picture and loop a piece of yarn or string for hanging the picture.

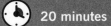 20 minutes

Velour Chi-Rho Bookmark

Grades 1–4

Materials:

Wide velour ribbon or velour paper	Glue
Scissors	Felt in a variety of colors
Pencils	Chi-Rho pattern (see page 75)

> ### FAITH CONNECTION
> *The Chi-Rho symbol is an ancient monogram of Christ. It appears on altars, bookmarks, and vestments. The monogram has been in Christian use for at least 1600 years. The symbol is derived from the first two letters of the Greek XPICTOC (pronounced "Christos"). The letters abbreviate the name of Christ.*

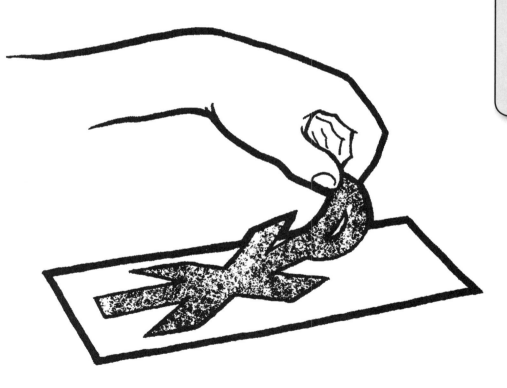

Directions:

1. Using the pattern, trace and cut a Chi-Rho from the velour.

2. Cut out a piece of felt to bookmark size, large enough to glue the Chi-Rho in the center with a felt border around it.

3. Glue the Chi-Rho onto the felt.

Velour Chi-Rho Bookmark Pattern

Yarn Art Creations

Grades 1–4

Materials:

Assorted colors of yarn	Construction paper or velour paper
Glue	Pencils
Scissors	Chi-Rho pattern (see page 77)
Crayons	

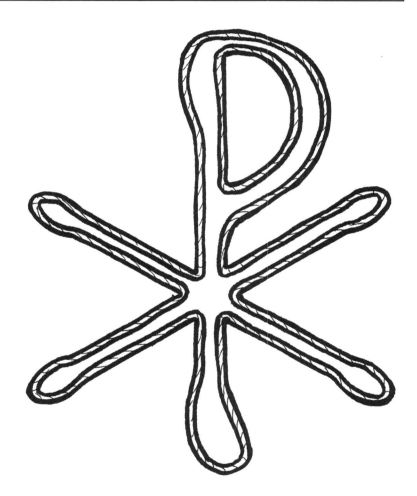

FAITH CONNECTION

The Chi-Rho symbol is an ancient monogram of Christ. It appears on altars, bookmarks, and vestments. The monogram has been in Christian use for at least 1600 years. The symbol is derived from the first two letters of the Greek XPICTOC (pronounced "Christos"). The letters abbreviate the name of Christ.

Directions:

1. Trace the Chi-Rho pattern on construction paper. Glue the yarn to the outline of the Chi-Rho.

2. Add details with the crayons.

3. If you use velour paper, use a larger piece of contrasting-colored construction paper on which to mount the velour.

Yarn Art Creations Pattern

Bloom Where You're Planted

Grades 1–8

Materials:

4" squares of green construction paper	7" squares of yellow construction paper
Green drinking straw	Glue
Plastic or paper cup	Paper clips
Orange and brown crayons	Pencils
Scissors	

> **FAITH CONNECTION**
>
> *Talk with the children about what it means when we say that a flower blooms. (It grows.) Explain that, like flowers, we are also called to bloom and grow into followers of Jesus.*

Directions:

1. Ask the children for words that tell how they can bloom where they're planted and bring Jesus' love to others. Write their words on the board so that the children can select from among them. (Examples: *serve, love, smile, care, pray, give, help, share, work, study, obey.*) Show the children a sample flower.

2. Fold the yellow square as shown in the picture on page 79. Cut the open edge to a point and open the flower.

3. Fold the green square in half, draw a leaf, and cut it out double as shown on page 79.

4. Use a brown crayon to write "I Will" on the center of one side of the flower and "Go to Mass" on the center of the other side.

5. Make brown specks around the writing on both sides of the center to represent a solid circle of seeds.

6. Outline the petals with an orange crayon.

7. Write a word on each petal to tell what you will do to bring Jesus' love to others. Write first in pencil and then go over the writing with orange crayon.

8. Write "Bloom Where You're Planted" twice on the other side of the flower, writing one word on each petal.

9. Glue the flower and leaves to the drinking straw. Glue the leaves about one third of the distance from the end of the stem so that you can place the stem into the cup.

10. Turn the cup over and use the point of a pencil to make a hole in the bottom center of the cup. Push the stem of the flower into the hole so that the flower stands upright. (If the children make the hole too large, place a paper clip in the back of the hole to support the stem.)

2.

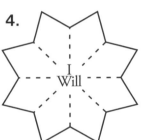

4.

7.    8.

9.

3.

Fish Mobile

Grades 1–8

Materials:

Green and purple poster board	Poster board in a third contrasting color
Wire or thread for mobile	Glue
Coat hanger	Patterns (see page 81)

You will need aides for children in grades 1 and 2.

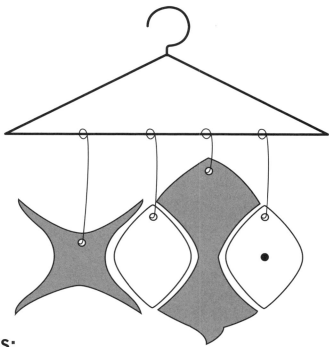

> ### FAITH CONNECTION
> *One of the earliest symbols used by Christians to represent Jesus Christ was the fish. It was a secret sign for early believers to identify themselves to each other because they were publicly persecuted for their belief in Jesus. Explain to the students that the Greek word for fish,* ichthus, *is formed from the first letters of the words* Jesus Christ, Son of God, Savior.

Before Class:

Make up an ample number of fish-segment patterns. For the younger students, trace the segments on the cardboard.

Directions:

1. Trace the fish-segment patterns on a piece of green poster board and on a piece of poster board of a contrasting color.

2. Cut out each segment individually. Glue the same-sized and same-shaped pieces of each color together so each piece is green on one side and the contrasting color on the other side.

3. Cut out scales in purple poster board and glue onto the green poster board.

4. Attach each segment to a length of thread or wire. Attach all four fish segments to a coat hanger for hanging.

Fish Mobile Patterns

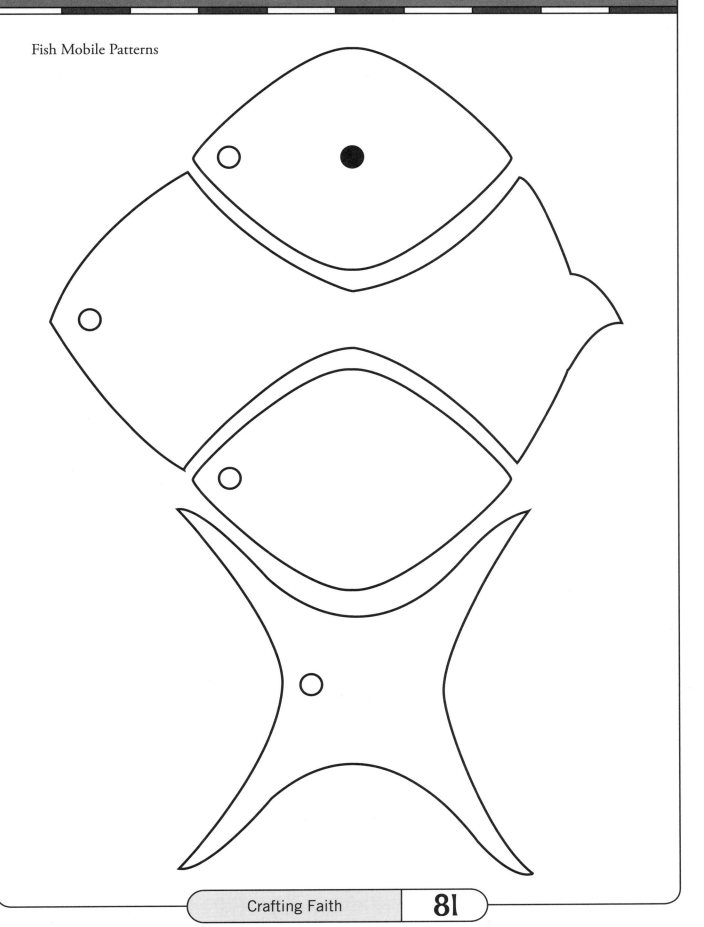

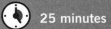 25 minutes

Easter Cross

Grades 3–8

Materials:

Scrap paper or newspaper	String
White paper	Artificial flowers
Scissors	Gold paint (optional)
Glue	

FAITH CONNECTION

Tell the children that, because of Jesus' Resurrection on Easter morning, the cross has become a symbol of victory over sin and death for us.

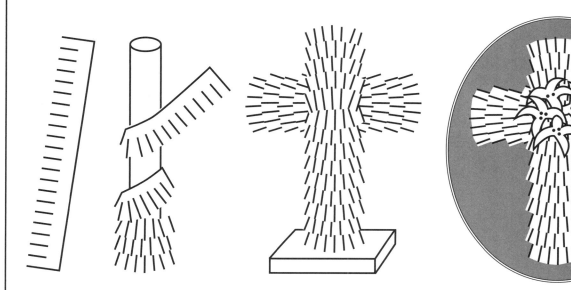

Directions:

1. Roll scrap paper or newspaper to make the beams of a cross.

2. Fringe strips of white paper. Curl the fringe with a scissor's edge. (You may spray the tips of the fringe with gold paint.)

3. Wrap the fringed strips around the beams. Glue or tie the beams together.

4. Add artificial flowers to the center of the cross.

5. Place the cross on a base or in a nest of Easter grass. The cross could also be mounted on a background.

🕐 **25 minutes**

Jesus' Name

Grades 1–8

Materials:

Jesus' name pattern, 1 for each student (see page 84)	Black fine-point, felt-tip pen (permanent)
Poster board	Masking tape
Rulers	

> **FAITH CONNECTION**
> *Tell the children that we are all called to recognize Jesus in our everyday lives. Explain that this project is an exercise in recognizing the name of Jesus.*

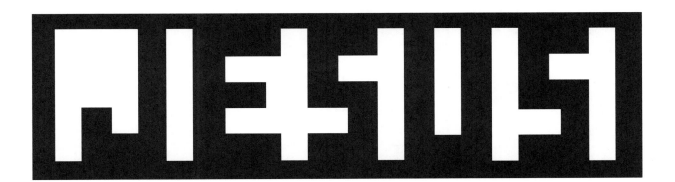

Before Class:

Have the pattern traced onto poster board for students in grades 1 and 2.

Directions:

1. Place pattern on poster board. Carefully trace pattern onto poster board. (You may wish to use masking tape to hold pattern to the poster board.)

4. Remove pattern.

5. Trace over the lines with felt-tip pen. Use a ruler if necessary.

6. Discover the name that you have made from the pattern is *Jesus*. Through all our liturgical seasons and every day, we are to follow Jesus.

Jesus' Name Pattern

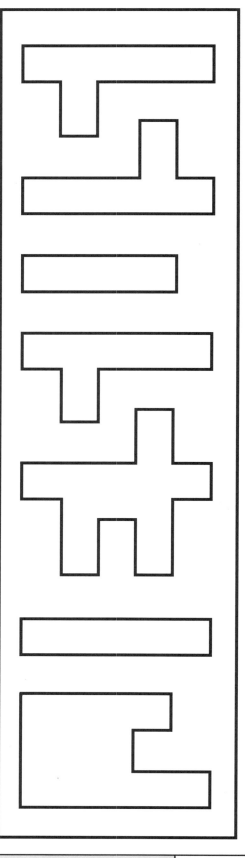

Jesus Quotation Plaque

Grades 1–8

Materials:

Copies of a quotation or Bible verse about Jesus	Poster board (5" x 6"), 1 per student
Glue	Paper punch
Crayons, colored pencils, markers	Yarn

"I am the good
shepherd, and
I know mine
and mine
know me"
–John 10:14

FAITH CONNECTION

Tell the children that one of the ways that Jesus speaks to us is through Scripture. Invite them to create a plaque that includes a Scripture quotation of Jesus or a Scripture verse about Jesus.

Directions:

1. Glue quotation or verse to the center of the poster board. Let it dry.

2. Decorate the plaque using crayons, colored pencils, or markers.

3. Punch a hole in the poster board. Thread a piece of yarn through the hole and tie it in a loop for hanging.

Paper Plate Sheep

Grades 1–4

Materials:

Paper plates, 1 dinner and 1 dessert plate for each child	A handful of cotton balls for each child
Black construction paper	Glue
Crayons or markers	Stapler
Patterns for ears, tails, and legs (see page 87)	

Before Class:

Prepare a sample of the completed sheep craft along with one set of materials for each child. Staple a dinner plate to a dessert plate to make the sheep's head and body. Out of black construction paper, cut triangles for ears and tails and rectangles for legs.

Directions:

1. Distribute the necessary materials to each child.
2. Help them glue the ears, legs, and a tail in place.
3. Have the children draw faces for their sheep on the small paper plate, using crayons or markers.
4. Have them glue cotton balls to the large paper plate to make the sheep's fleece.
5. Help the children write their names on their sheep.

FAITH CONNECTION

The Parable of the Good Shepherd (John 10:11–16) expresses the relationship of love and trust that is possible between humans and Christ. Although few children today have experiences with sheep or shepherds, this parable still interests them. It evokes a sense of peace and inner joy, indicating that the Christian message can satisfy deep needs. Children can relate God's love, as manifested through the Good Shepherd figure, to the love they experience through other people. Although the children will gradually appreciate the meaning of the parable, their eventual understanding of it is facilitated by their early appreciation of it.

Paper Plate Sheep Patterns for ears and legs

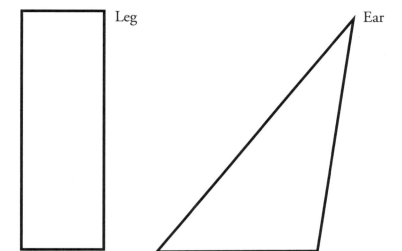

Leg

Ear

Crayon-on-Chalk Transfer Etching

Grades 1–8

Materials:

Newspapers	Sharp pencil
Two sheets of manila or white drawing paper identical in size for each student	INRI pattern
Yellow chalk	Optional: Crayons or paints, brushes, and scissors
Dark crayon	

FAITH CONNECTION

Show the children a crucifix with the letters INRI *above Jesus' head. Explain that the initials* INRI *represent the title "Jesus the Nazorean, the King of the Jews" in Latin (John 19:19), which Pontius Pilate placed over the head of the crucified Jesus to mock him.*

INRI

Directions:

1. Cover a work surface with newspaper. Cover one of the sheets of drawing paper with a heavy coat of yellow chalk.

2. Apply a heavy layer of dark crayon so the chalk is completely covered.

3. Lay the clean sheet of paper over the sheet covered with crayon. Using your sharp pencil, trace an *INRI* pattern onto the uncolored sheet. Press hard, working on a hard surface so that the transfer etching will be clear. You may shade the inside of the letters or design the letters in various ways.

4. When you remove the top sheet, you will find that the pencil drawing has caused the crayon wax to leave the chalk backing.

Optional: For younger children, use the block letters *INRI* or other design and copy one for each student. Let them color or paint the letters. They could also cut out each letter and paste it onto a darker sheet of construction paper.

Bible Story Diorama

Grades 3–8

Materials:

Shoebox	Cardboard
Scraps of fabric	Glue and tape
Colored paper	Scissors
Clay or play dough	Pencils

> **FAITH CONNECTION**
> *Show the children a Bible and point out how the life of Jesus is found in the Gospels of Matthew, Mark, Luke, and John. Invite them to work on a project that shows a scene from the life of Jesus.*

Directions:

1. Have a group of students work on a project together or have them work individually. Have the students decide which scene of Jesus' life they are going to portray.

2. Decorate the inside of the shoebox with scraps of fabric or paper.

3. Using clay, shape the characters in the story. Place the figures in the shoebox

Optional: Students may use toy figures instead of clay.

⏱ **30 minutes**

mosaic

Grades 3–8

Materials:

Patterns (see page 90–91)	Heavy cardboard, size 5" × 7"
Black yarn	White glue or other clear-drying glue
Aquarium gravel of various colors	

> **FAITH CONNECTION**
> *Explain to the children that the cross and the Chi-Rho are two of the most cherished symbols of Jesus Christ. (An explanation of the Chi-Rho can be found on page 74 and page 76.)*

Directions:

1. Trace one of the patterns onto the cardboard or design your own. Using white glue, outline the pattern with the black yarn.

2. Fill in the pattern using various colors of aquarium gravel. Set the gravel by using white glue.

3. Let the mosaic dry 24 hours before taking it home.

Mosaic Pattern

Chi-Rho Patterns

Bread of Life Magnet

Grades 5–8

Materials:

Brown construction paper	Magnetic strip tape
Bread patterns (see page 94)	White craft or fabric glue
Large alphabet macaroni noodles (#18 size)	Tiny dried flowers
Ribbon, needle, and thread to sew bow	Optional: Toothpicks
Roll of burlap strips (1 1/2" wide)	

> **FAITH CONNECTION**
> *Read or summarize the story of Jesus' multiplying of the loaves and fish in John 6:1–15. Point out that when the people asked Jesus to continue feeding them with this bread, Jesus replied, "I am the bread of life" (John 6:35).*

Before Class:

1. Cut brown construction paper into shape of a slice of bread.

2. Cut burlap strips into 8" pieces.

Directions:

1. In the middle of the burlap strip, glue two or three flowers.

2. Glue construction paper bread slices over stems of flowers, carefully pressing burlap to back of bread. Glue well.

3. Arrange letters on the bread. Glue to the bread. Toothpicks may be helpful to place letters. Suggested wording: "I am the Bread of Life," "Give us this day our daily bread," "Bread broken, bread shared."

4. Glue or sew ribbon to the top of the burlap.

5. Attach two small pieces of magnetic tape to the back of the burlap behind the bow.

Bread of Life Magnet Patterns

8" Strip

Piece of Bread

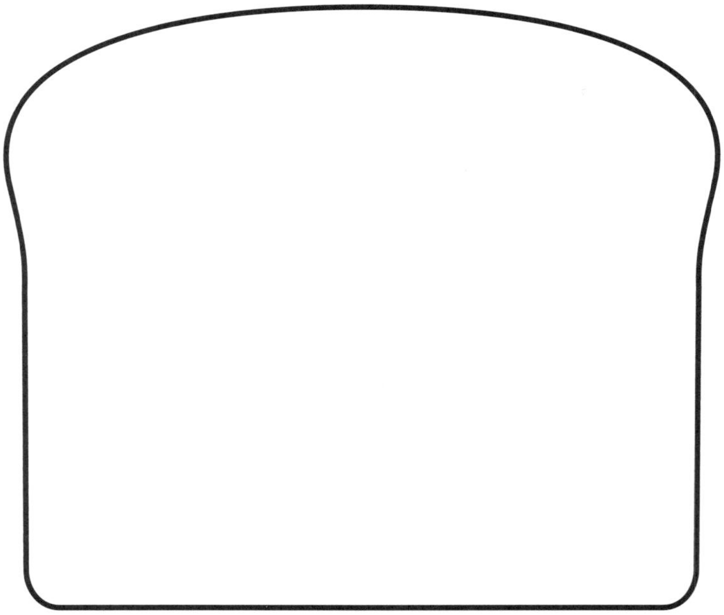

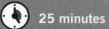 25 minutes

Tele-Viewer

Grades 5–8

Materials:

Square cardboard box or carton, 1 per student	Roll of white paper, 1 per student
Pencil	Knife
Watercolor paints or crayons	Cardboard tube from paper towels, 2 per student
Scissors	Tape
Ruler	

FAITH CONNECTION

Show the children a Bible and point out how the life of Jesus is found in the Gospels of Matthew, Mark, Luke, and John. Invite them to work on a project that shows a scene from the life of Jesus.

You may suggest the events of the Christmas story, Jesus' ministry, or his death and Resurrection. Brainstorm Bible stories that the students particularly like. If the Christmas story is used, play or sing a familiar Christmas carol as background music while doing this project.

Directions:

1. Remove the front section of the box and discard.

2. Draw a line 1" in on each side and 1" from bottom.

3. Cut along this line to make "slots" for the paper to slide through.

4. Along the entire roll of paper, paint story scenes from any part of the life of Christ, allowing each picture to be "framed" in the center section of the box.

5. Tape or glue the ends of the roll of paper to the cardboard tube.

6. Insert the story scene and unroll the pictures as the story unfolds.

7. As the story proceeds, have each student take a turn narrating what is happening in each frame of the story.

Christmas Card Holder

Grades 1–8

Materials:

Shoe box	Christmas tinsel or ribbon
Contact paper or construction paper	Christmas stickers
Glue	

Directions:

1. Cover the box with contact paper or construction paper.

2. Write "God bless our friends and family" or "We are thankful for friends and family" on the box.

3. Decorate the box with tinsel or ribbon and stickers.

4. After the children make this delightful holder for their families' Christmas cards, send home a note encouraging families to keep the holder on or near their dinner table. Each night they can choose a card to read as a family and share the meaning and illustration on the card. Then they can pray for the people or person who sent them the card.

Christmas Nativity Ornament

Grades 1–8

Materials:

Plastic container lids or poster board	Glue
Star pattern (see page 98)	Sticker or small picture (such as a prayer card) of the Nativity
Clear glitter	Paper punch

> **FAITH CONNECTION**
>
> *Write the word* Nativity *on the board and explain to the children that we use this word to refer to the birth of Jesus.*

Before Class:

Use the star pattern to cut out stars from the plastic lids or poster board and punch holes in the top of each.

Directions:

1. Have the children put the Nativity sticker or glue the Nativity picture on the plastic or poster board star.

2. Place small amounts of glue all around the star and sprinkle clear glitter over the entire star.

Christmas Nativity Ornament Pattern

 20 minutes

Holy Spirit Necklace

Grades 1–5

Materials:

Poster board dove (with hole punched), 1 per student (see page 100)	Shirt, smock, or apron to protect clothing
Twine	Newspapers
Acrylic or tempera paint	Felt-tip pens, markers and/ or crayons
Small brushes	

FAITH CONNECTION

Say the prayer "Come Holy Spirit, fill the hearts of the faithful and renew the face of the earth." Remind the students to wear the necklace they will be making as a sign to others that they share God's life-giving Spirit. As they care for others, they will be renewing the face of the earth.

Before Class:

For the younger students, print the words "Renew the face of the earth" on the dove.

Directions:

1. Cover the tables with newspapers. Have the students wear protective shirts.

2. Have the students write the words "Renew the face of the earth" very carefully on the dove.

3. Let the students decorate their doves with paint. They may also use felt-tip pens or crayons.

4. Push the twine through the hole and make a knot. Use a length of twine 18" to 20" as the "chain" for the necklace.

Holy Spirit Necklace Pattern

Holy Spirit Necklace

Fruit of the Spirit Tree

Grades 4–8

Materials:

Construction or rice paper (12" × 16")	Tissue or crepe paper in various colors
Black tempera paint for tree trunk	Old magazines
Green, yellow, orange tempera paint for leaves	Black felt-tip pens
Straws	Water
Shirt, smock, or apron to protect clothing	Container for mixing paint and water
Small piece of sponge	Crayons
Clip-type clothespins	Pencils
Optional: Small paintbrushes	

Before Class:

Write the verse from Galatians 5:22 on the board. Underline the fruits described or list the fruits the Holy Spirit wishes to produce in us. You may wish to make up fruit shapes with the literal/spiritual fruits written on them for grades 1 and 2. Students may glue or paste the fruit to the tree.

Directions:

1. Cover tables well with newspapers.

2. Thin down black tempera paint (1/2 paint and 1/2 water).

3. Drop a blob of this black paint on bottom half of paper.

4. Blow through the straw to "move" the paint to make a tree. Keep blowing to make more branches.

FAITH CONNECTION

Read Galatians 5:22 from the Bible. This project can be used to help students get in touch with the Holy Spirit as a special presence in the life of each person who is following the example of Jesus. Use straws to "paint" a tree. Help the students understand the concept of the Holy Spirit by showing them that when they blow through the straw, they cannot really see their breath, but can see the results as their breath moves the paint. The power of the Holy Spirit is a lot like their unseen breath that has the power to move the paint on the paper. We cannot see the Holy Spirit, but we can experience the results of what happens when we cooperate with the love of God.

5. To make leaves, pinch a piece of sponge with a clothespin. Using the clothespin as a handle, dip the sponge into the green, yellow, or orange tempera paint and "sponge" on leaves.

Some other ideas for leaves are (a) using a small paintbrush and tempera paint, dot and/or swirl the brush on the paper; (b) twist little pieces of tissue or crepe paper and glue or paste to branches; (c) cut out leaves of fruit or flowers from magazines and glue or paste to branches; (d) cut out pictures from magazines that show examples of people doing good things that symbolize the "fruit of the Spirit" and paste onto branches. Examples are Love—mother and child or a family hugging; Joy—balloons, smiling and laughing faces; Peace—sunset, lake, tiny animal asleep.

6. Let dry.

7. Add "fruit" to the tree by writing the following words at the top of the branches or among the leaves: *Love, Joy, Peace, Patience, Kindness, Goodness, Faithfulness, Gentleness, Self-Control.* Use a pencil, black felt-tip-pen, or crayons to write the words.

8. Mount the tree picture on another piece of construction paper to make a frame. Title your painting "Fruit of the Spirit Tree."

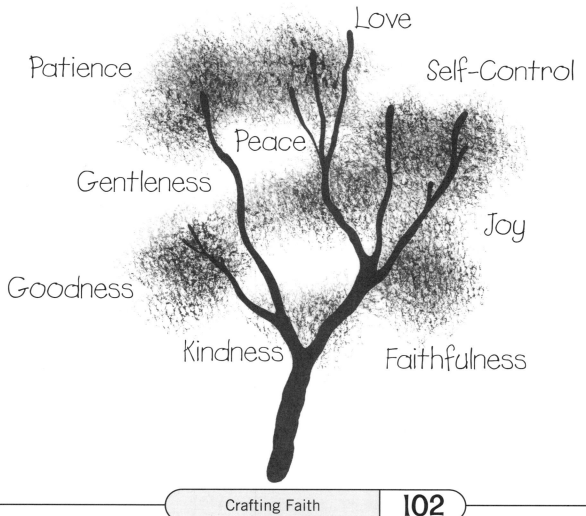

Suncatchers

Grades 1–8

Materials:

Crayon shavings	Newspapers
Wax paper	String
Acrylic or tempera paint	Iron and ironing board
Patterns (see page 103)	Optional: Dark construction paper, glue

You will want to use aides with the younger students.

> **FAITH CONNECTION**
> *The Holy Spirit is God's presence within us. "I will give you a new heart and place a new spirit within you" (Ezekiel 36:26–27). Our attitude and actions are shaped by the loving presence of the Holy Spirit that is God's life within us.*

Before Class:

Prepare patterns and make samples for the students to see.

Directions:

1. Spread newspapers over working surface.

2. Place a pattern on the newspaper to serve as a guide.

3. Lay a piece of clear kitchen wax paper on top of the newspaper according to the size desired.

4. Drop shavings of crayons onto the wax paper, keeping within the lines of the pattern.

5. Lay another piece of wax paper on top of the crayon shavings.

6. Place the sandwiched sheets between layers of newspaper and press with a warm iron for a stained-glass effect. Only adults should do the ironing.

7. Mat with or glue on dark construction paper or display in a window by trimming around the symbol and attaching a string for hanging.

Suncathers Patterns

Crayon Etching

Grades 4–8

Materials:

White paper	Black crayon
Crayons in a number of bright colors	Pen for etching
Optional: Scratch-Art® rainbow paper	

FAITH CONNECTION

Ask the students if they know how many apostles Jesus had (twelve) *and if they can name any of them (see* Matthew 10:2–4; Mark 3:16–19; *or* Luke 6:14–16*).*

Directions:

1. Use several different bright colors of crayons to completely cover the white paper in a rainbow or other pattern.

2. Color over the paper with black crayon. If you prefer, use Scratch-Art® rainbow paper.

3. Use a pen to etch a picture on the paper. One idea is to etch a picture of the Holy Spirit descending upon the apostles on Pentecost.

4. At the bottom of the etching, the older students can list the names of the apostles.

Potted Plants

Grades 1–4

Materials:

Small paper cup, 1 per student	Vegetable or flower seeds of any variety
Potting soil	Rags for cleanup

> **FAITH CONNECTION**
>
> *Read to the children John 12:24. Tell them that Jesus used the image of a grain of wheat dying in order to bear fruit to explain how he must die in order to rise again. Explain that planting a seed to grow a plant reminds us of Jesus' Resurrection.*

Directions:

1. Have the students use the newspapers to cover their work surface.

2. Give a paper cup and seeds to each student.

3. Pass out the potting soil and have the students plant the seeds.

4. Water the soil slightly and have the students care for the seeds at home by putting the potted seeds on a window sill and watering them regularly.

He Is Risen: An Empty Egg

Materials:

Paper plates, 2 per student	Scissors
Crayons	Paper fastener

FAITH CONNECTION

Read or summarize the story of Jesus' Resurrection from Luke 24:1–8.

Directions:

1. Use light-colored crayons to decorate the outside of one plate to look like an Easter egg.

2. Cut the first plate in half. Fasten the sides to the bottom center of the second plate with a paper fastener as shown.

3. Open up the egg and write "He Is Risen" on the bottom plate.

4. Show your Easter egg to others to share the message of the angel on that first Easter morning.

Suggestions:

1. If you wish, decorate the outside of the bottom plate too.

2. Use stickers or markers to decorate your egg.

3. Wet the plate with water, then put colored bits of tissue paper over it. Remove the tissue when dry.

4. Glue on pieces of colored tissue paper with a mixture of water and white glue.

Butterfly

Grades 1–4

Materials:

Pattern (see page 109)	Glitter
Glue	Chenille wire or craft stems
4½" square sheets of white paper	Colored tissue or crepe paper

FAITH CONNECTION

Talk about why a butterfly is seen as a symbol of Jesus' Resurrection: The caterpillar goes into a cocoon and is transformed into a beautiful butterfly. The cocoon symbolizes the grave from which Jesus rose, transformed into the risen Christ.

Directions:

1. Using the pattern provided, cut butterfly wings on the fold line from a 4½" square of folded paper.

2. Decorate the wings and apply glue. Shake on glitter.

3. Bend the chenille wire in half, slip wings between wire, and gather the colored paper in the bend of the wire.

4. Twist the ends of the wire to make antennae for the butterfly.

Butterfly Pattern

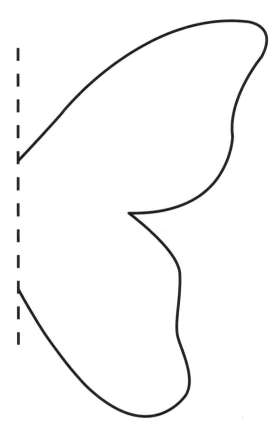

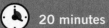 20 minutes

Butterfly Prayer

Grades 1–8

Materials:

Unlined paper	Pens, pencils, or markers
Ruler	Butterfly patter (see page 111)

FAITH CONNECTION
Children should be encouraged to pray to God in their own words. One interesting way to teach spontaneous prayer at Easter time is with the following butterfly prayer activity.

Before Class:

Draw an outline of a butterfly widthwise to cover an entire unlined standard-size sheet of paper. Inside the butterfly, draw horizontal lines, using a pen and ruler. On the top line, print the words "My Easter Prayer." You now have a sheet of butterfly stationery! Duplicate one sheet for each student in the class.

Directions:

1. Ask the students to write short, individual, Easter-themed prayers on their butterfly stationery. Also, tell the children to sign their names. A butterfly prayer may be something like this.

   My Easter Prayer

   Hi God!

   Thank you for Jesus.

   I like Easter and spring.

   Alleluia.

   Love, Kelly

2. When the students are finished, call on volunteers to share their prayers with the class.

3. The butterfly prayers can be used as an offering at a prayer service or taken home to be shared with parents.

Butterfly Prayer Pattern

Resurrection Shadow Picture

Grades 1–8

FAITH CONNECTION
Remind the children that the Resurrection of Jesus is the most important part of our faith.

Materials:

9" aluminum pie pan, 1 per student	Black rickrack or braid
Black felt	Hanger
Glue	Pattern (see page 113)

You will need aides for grades 1 and 2.

Directions:

1. Using the pattern provided, cut out a silhouette of the risen Christ from black felt. Cut out several clouds from black felt.

2. Glue the silhouette of Christ and the clouds on the inside of the pie pan.

3. Glue rickrack or braid around the edge of the pan to make a frame.

4. Glue a hanger on the back. The hanger can be purchased or made from cardboard with a hole punched in one end.

Shadow Pattern

Handy Easter Lilies

Grades 1–4

Materials:

White construction paper	Tape or stapler
Pencils	Green craft stem
Scissors	

FAITH CONNECTION

The white Easter lily fills the church on Easter morning as a sign that Christ has risen. Here is an idea that uses hands to create this Easter flower symbol.

Directions:

1. Have the children trace their hands on construction paper and cut them out.

2. Roll each paper hand so that the pinky meets the thumb, then tape or staple them together.

3. Secure a green craft stem at the bottom opening (where the wrist would be) of each paper hand. The result will resemble a lily.

or

 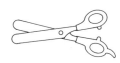 

Materials:

White construction paper	Brown pipe cleaner
Tape	Pencil
Green pipe cleaner	Paper cup or pastel-colored sheet of paper

Directions:

1. Use the pencil to trace the child's hand onto the white construction paper.

2. Cut out the hand shape and roll the pinky so it meets the thumb. Secure in place with a piece of tape.

3. Through the bottom opening (where the wrist would be), slide a green pipe cleaner to form the stem of the flower. Hook the top of the green pipe cleaner to make the stamen of the flower.

4. The finished flower may be placed in a vase (paper cup) or glued to a pastel colored sheet of paper with the message "Christ is risen."

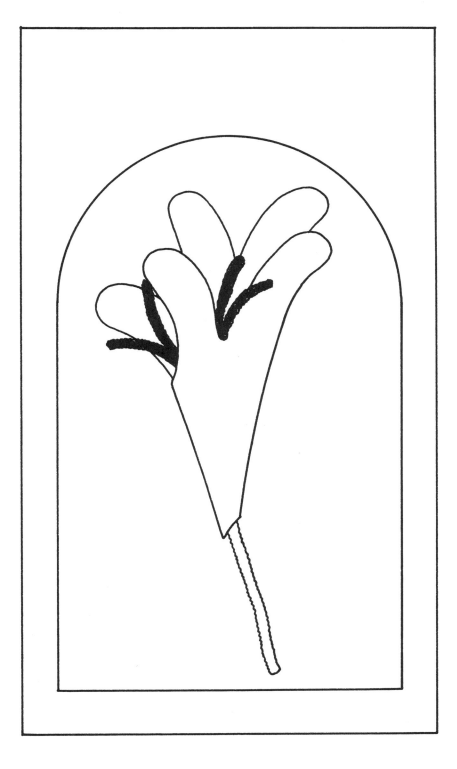

Easter Lilies

Grades 5–8

Materials:

Strips of plain, unlined white paper twice as long as they are wide	Scissors
Glue	

1.

2.

3. 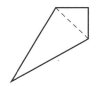   **4.**

5. & 6.

Directions:

1. Fold each strip of paper in half to form a square.

2. Then fold it again into thirds from the corner on the fold.

3. Cut off the point and cut the flower petals.

4. Open the paper.

5. Curl each petal with a scissors blade.

6. Overlap petals A and B and glue the two together.

Optional: If you wish, glue a yellow strip in the center to make a stamen and cut a few green leaves.

Part 1: From Cocoons to Butterflies

Grades 5–8

Materials:

2" wide slips of note paper	Paste-and-water mixture or flour-and-water mixture
Newsprint in strips	Sponge
Tray	Paper towels
Water	Pencil or pen

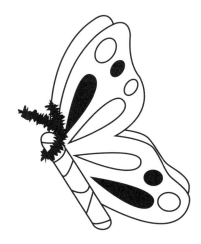

Directions:

1. Direct the students to write a letter to Jesus, telling him what they plan to do during Lent to change themselves into better persons. Use small slips of paper, about 2" wide. Suggest positive actions of helping others.

2. Roll up the finished letters.

3. Dip strips of newsprint in a paste mixture or a flour mixture, then wrap the strips around each rolled-up letter. Several strips are needed for each letter.

4. The little "cocoons" may then be placed on a cookie tray to dry. A slip of paper on which the student's name is written may be placed under his or her cocoon for later identification. The cocoons will dry in a few days into hard shells.

5. Clean hands and work areas with water, sponge, and paper towels.

Part ll: From Cocoons to Butterflies

Grades 5–8

Materials:

White construction paper	Scissors
Crayons	Pins
Butterfly pattern (see page 119)	Chenille wire or craft stems

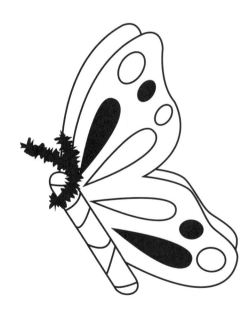

Directions:

1. Trace the butterfly pattern onto white construction paper.
2. Color and cut out the butterflies.
3. Color the body of the cocoon.
4. Attach the cocoon to the body with pins.
5. Twist a pipe cleaner around the body, just under the head. Twist to make antennae.

Note: Put the student's name on the back of his or her butterfly if the butterflies are to be distributed later.

FAITH CONNECTION

Talk about how the students made cocoons in which the students placed notes to Jesus stating what they would do during Lent to help change themselves into better persons to become more loving persons. The caterpillar in the cocoon is transformed into a beautiful butterfly, into a new kind of life.

Discuss the fact that when Jesus died and was buried, he also changed into a new kind of life with God. We say that he rose from the dead.

Tell the students that perhaps in this past month they changed a small part of themselves as they tried to be loving to others. If they failed, they can try again. Ask the students to keep the butterfly as a reminder of this challenge.

From Cocoons to Butterflies Pattern

Lighthouse

Grades 1–8

Materials:

Paper towel roll or potato-chip can	Enlarged and printed lighthouse copy
Tape	Yellow paper strips
Markers	

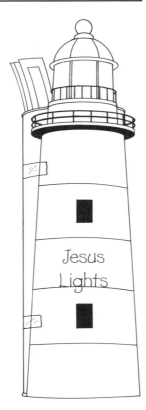

> ### FAITH CONNECTION
>
> *Jesus lights our way. Jesus called himself the Light of the World (John 8:12).*
>
> *Make a lighthouse and discuss how Jesus lights the way for us in life. Fill the lighthouse with ways the family can grow closer in faith.*

Directions:

1. Have the children cut out the lighthouse picture and color it.

2. Tape the lighthouse around the paper towel roll or potato-chip can.

3. On yellow paper strips, print out the following suggestions for families. Invite them to take one idea a week from the lighthouse and work on it together. Some possible suggestions

   Read a Bible story together right after supper or at bedtime.

   Take a walk and talk about the wonder of God's creation.

   Begin recycling something you have not yet started to recycle.

   Clean out your closets and drawers and take a trip to the Goodwill.

   Bake cookies together and give some of them away.

Say It with Tambourines

Materials:

Paper plates, 2 per student	Crayons or felt-tip markers
Paper punch	Yarn
Jingle-style bells, 12 per student	

> **FAITH CONNECTION**
> *Read Psalm 150:1–6 and talk about the various instruments that are mentioned as ways of giving praise to God. Invite the children to make an instrument with which to praise God.*

Directions:

1. Hold the faces of two paper plates together and punch twelve holes around the edges.

2. Use a piece of yarn to tie a bell at each hole.

3. Use crayons or markers to decorate.

4. Pray Psalm 150 together and make a joyful noise with the tambourines.

Rhythm Maracas

Grades 1–4

Materials:

Salt carton	Construction paper
Dried beans	Dowel rod
Tape	Optional: Yarn for decorating

FAITH CONNECTION

Read Psalm 150:1–6 and talk about the various instruments that are mentioned as ways of giving praise to God. Invite the children to make an instrument with which to praise God.

Directions:

1. Put a few dried beans in an empty salt carton. Tape the carton shut.

2. Cover the carton with construction paper.

3. For the handle, make a hole in the top and bottom of the carton and push a dowel rod through the carton.

4. Sing a happy song about God's goodness and play the maracas to accompany the singing.

Optional: Tie pieces of yarn on one end of the dowel rod.

Alternative: Invite the children to make rhythm maracas to add to the celebration of the Mass. Distribute two plastic cups and a handful of dried beans to each child. Guide the children to put the beans in one cup. Then have them place the second cup upside down on top of the first cup. Help the children tape the cups together. Then wrap the maracas in aluminum foil or plastic wrap. Invite the children to decorate their maracas and write their names on them. You might encourage the children to shake their maracas when singing songs during a lesson.

Angelus Felt Picture

Grades 4–8

Materials:

Felt material for background	Various colors of felt material for the patterns
Picture frame	Pencils
Glue	Scissors
Cardboard	Patterns (see page 124)

FAITH CONNECTION

Explain to the children that Catholics pray a traditional prayer called the Angelus each day at noon. Point out that this prayer begins with the words "The Angel of the Lord declared unto Mary. And she conceived of the Holy Spirit."

Before Class:

Precut picture pieces and felt pieces for the younger students.

Directions:

1. For each picture piece, trace a pattern on the felt, using the pattern provided.
2. Fit picture to the frame size.
3. Cut colored felt into pieces. Use gold for the halo, blue for the gown, etc.
4. Glue to felt material background and insert the finished picture into the frame.

Angelus Felt Picture Patterns

Flowers

Stems

Halos

Angel
Body

Angel
Hair

Hands

Mary
Body

Sun

Faces

Wing

Wing

Prayer of St. Francis

Grades 3–8

Materials:

Magazines for pictures of birds and animals	Copies of the Peace Prayer of St. Francis, 1 per student
Poster board	Paper punch
Scissors	Yarn
Glue	

> **FAITH CONNECTION**
> *Talk with the children about how St. Francis of Assisi was known for his great love of animals and for his Peace Prayer.*

Directions:

1. Cut out pictures of birds and animals from the magazines.
2. Glue the pictures and the prayer on poster board.
3. Punch a hole in the poster board. Thread a piece of yarn through the hole and tie it in a loop for hanging.

Peace Prayer of St. Francis

Lord, make me an instrument of your peace:

where there is hatred, let me sow love;

where there is injury, pardon;

where there is doubt, faith;

where there is despair, hope;

where there is darkness, light;

where there is sadness, joy.

O divine Master, grant that I may not so much seek

to be consoled as to console,

to be understood as to understand,

to be loved as to love.

For it is in giving that we receive,

it is in pardoning that we are pardoned,

it is in dying that we are born to eternal life. Amen

Peace Prayer of St. Francis

Lord, make me an instrument of your peace:
where there is hatred, let me sow love;
where there is injury, pardon;
where there is doubt, faith;
where there is despair, hope;
where there is darkness, light; a
where there is sadness, joy.

O divine Master, grant that I may
    not so much seek
to be consoled as to console,
to be understood as to understand,
to be loved as to love.
For it is in giving that we receive,
it is in pardoning that we are pardoned,
it is in dying that we are born to eternal life. Amen.

Starburst Cross

Grades 5–8

Materials:

Poster board	White glue
Pencils	Brushes
Scissors	Gold paint
Toothpicks (round)	

> **FAITH CONNECTION**
> *Remind the children that the cross is one of the most sacred images of the Christian faith.*

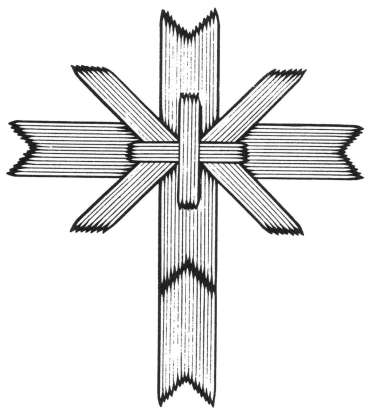

Directions:

1. On poster board, draw a cross about 7" long with 1¼" wide cross bars. Cut out the cross.

2. Brush on a coat of glue and place toothpicks as shown in the drawing. See page 128.

3. Glue toothpicks to arms.

4. Add another "cross" of toothpicks over the first one.

5. When the cross is dry, paint with gold paint.

Starburst Cross Pattern

1.

2.

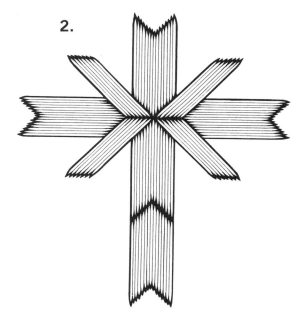

3.

Liturgical Calendar

Grades 1–8

Materials:

Colored pencils or crayons	Old Christmas and Easter cards
Copies of the liturgical calendar (see page 130)	Scissors
Magazines	Glue

> **FAITH CONNECTION**
> *Explain to the children that all time belongs to God and that Catholics strive to keep all time holy by following a liturgical calendar that recalls important events in the lives of Jesus, Mary, and the saints.*

Before Class:

Prepare ample patterns for younger students.

Directions:

1. Pass out copies of the liturgical calendar.

2. Have the students draw the symbols for each season on their liturgical calendar. (You may wish to list the seasons and their symbols on a chalkboard and provide patterns for the younger students.)

3. Older students should be able to determine for themselves what symbol applies to each liturgical season. Students may draw liturgical symbols on the appropriate season.

4. Students may cut out pictures from magazines, old Christmas cards, and Easter cards to paste on their liturgical calendar.

   ADVENT: Advent Wreath, Candle

   CHRISTMAS: Star, Nativity Scene, Manger, Gift Box

   LENT: Cross, Crown of Thorns, Palms

   EASTER: Lily, Candle, Plant, Butterfly, Lamb

   ORDINARY TIME: Tree, Vine and Branches

Liturgical Calendar Pattern

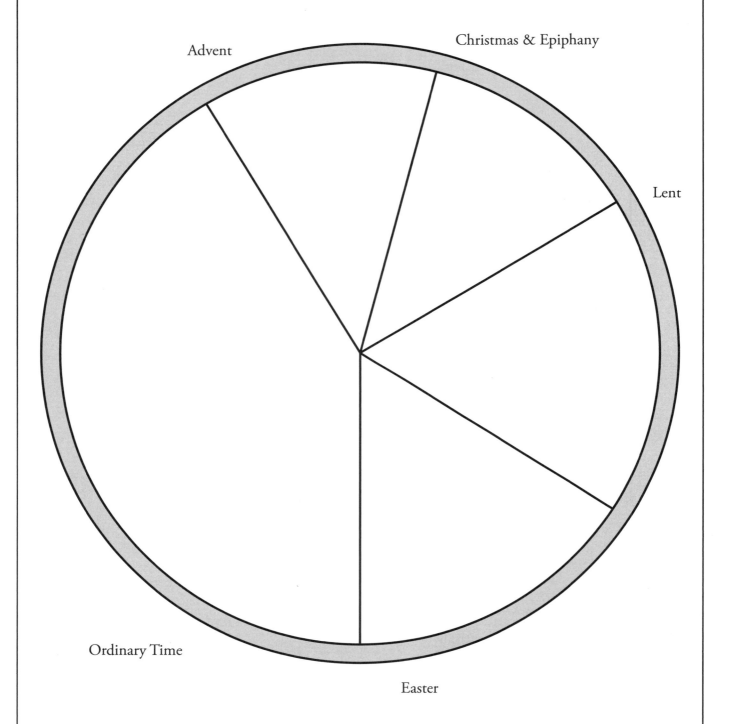

Advent

Christmas & Epiphany

Lent

Ordinary Time

Easter

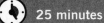

Rosary Poster

Grades 1–4

Materials:

Large poster board	Round "confetti" (use paper punch on construction paper)
Glue	Pencil
Crayons	Diagram of rosary (see page 132)

Diagram of rosary (see page 132)

> **FAITH CONNECTION**
> *October 7 is the Feast of Our Lady of the Rosary. A rosary is a set of beads (or knots) to help people pray the Our Father and Hail Mary prayers in five decades while remembering the events in the life of Jesus and Mary. The months of October and May are the two months especially devoted to Mary.*

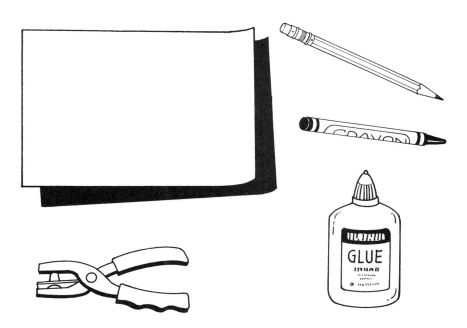

Before Class:

Make up bags of confetti. Pencil in the rosary on the poster board for grades 1 and 2.
Make an "x" or "o" where students are to glue dots (beads).

Directions:

1. Lightly pencil in a drawing of a rosary.
2. Glue confetti in appropriate places.
3. Draw a cross with the crayons.

Rosary Pattern

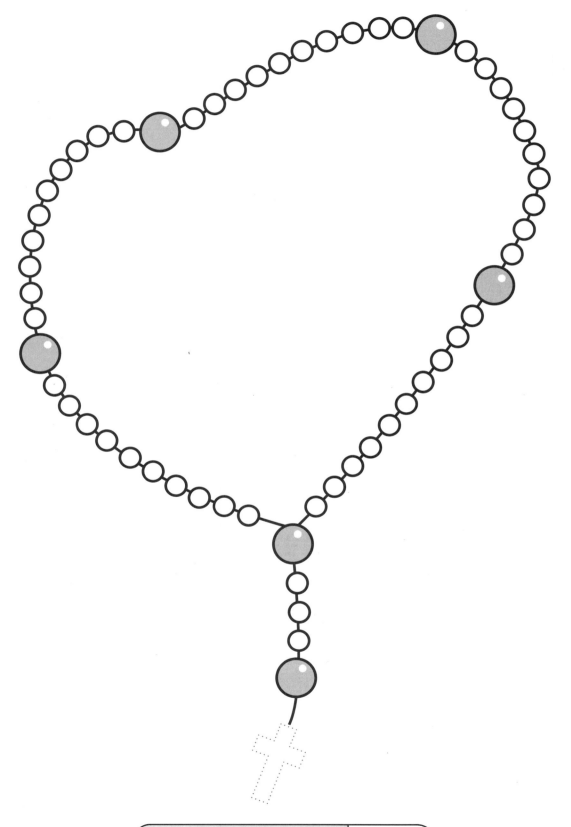

Rosary Activity Center

Grades 1–8

Materials:

Each rosary kit will need the following:	53 beads of one color for each Hail Mary
1 crucifix	6 beads of a different color for each Our Father
1 piece of cord with a dot marked 6" from one end	1 zip-top plastic bag
1 toothpick	Clear nail polish or craft glue

FAITH CONNECTION
Make the treasured prayer of the Rosary even more precious by praying it on a rosary that you and your family have made with your own hands and hearts.

Before Class:

This will take several class periods to complete. You will need to put a kit together for each student, consisting of all the materials needed to make the rosary, placed in a plastic bag. You should have a sample to show the class what a completed rosary looks like.

Directions:

1. Have each student select a bag of supplies. Each kit will include 53 beads of one color for each Hail Mary, 6 beads of a different color for each Our Father, one crucifix, and a piece of cord with a dot marked six inches from one end.

2. Sort the Hail Mary beads into 5 groups of 10 and one group of 3. Put the 6 Our Father beads together. Stretch out the piece of cord, straightening out any kinks.

3. Find the dot on the cord and tie a knot there. (See tip below.)

4. String 10 Hail Mary beads onto the long end of the cord. Slide them down so that they line up above the knot.

5. Tie another knot above the 10 beads, leaving a little space for them to slide.

6. Add an Our Father bead and tie another knot.

7. Continue the three previous steps until you have 5 sets of 10 beads but don't add the fifth Our Father bead yet.

8. Tie a knot at the end. Then, tie both ends together, forming a circle of beads. Pull that knot tight. Dab a little adhesive or clear nail polish on the knot to secure it.

9. Add one Our Father bead to the longer piece of cord.

10. Tie a knot and then add three Hail Mary beads.

11. Tie a knot, add the last Our Father bead, and tie another knot.

12. Secure the crucifix by tying a double knot. Pull the knot tight and dab a little adhesive or clear nail polish on it.

13. Once the adhesive or nail polish is dry, clip off the excess cords, hold your rosary, and say a prayer for your family.

14. You may wish to have your rosary blessed by a priest.

How to tie knots: First, determine where you want the knot to be. Second, make a loose knot near that point. Take the tip of a toothpick and, threading through the loose knot, press down on the spot on the cord where you want to place the knot. Then gently slide and tighten the loose knot around the point of the toothpick.

Diagram:

Use the diagram on page 136 with the instruction sheet to make a family rosary. The numbers on this diagram refer to the numbered instructions above.

3. Starting knot

4. Proceed in this direction

5. Knot

6. Knot

7. (Repeat steps 2, 3, and 4 for each section.)
Knot
Knot
Knot
Knot
Knot
Knot

8. Knot

9. Knot

10. Knot

11. Knot
Knot

12. Double knot
Six-inch starting cord (Clip at step 13.)
Excess ending cord (Clip at step 13.)

Prayers:

The Rosary is a prayer that engages both the hands and the heart. The feel of the rosary beads and the repetition of the prayers soothe and prepare us to open our hearts to God. Each mystery tells a story from the lives of Jesus and Mary. Praying the Rosary helps us share in their experiences. See page 139 for a visual guide to praying the Rosary with a rosary.

1. Pray the Sign of the Cross and the Apostles' Creed.
2. Pray the Our Father.
3. Pray 3 Hail Marys and 1 Glory Be to the Father.
4. Think about the first mystery. Pray the Our Father.
5. Pray 10 Hail Marys and 1 Glory Be to the Father.
6. Think about the second mystery. Pray the Our Father.
7. Pray 10 Hail Marys and 1 Glory Be to the Father.
8. Think about the third mystery. Pray the Our Father.
9. Pray 10 Hail Marys and 1 Glory Be to the Father.
10. Think about the fourth mystery. Pray the Our Father.
11. Pray 10 Hail Marys and 1 Glory Be to the father.
12. Think about the fifth mystery. Pray the Our Father.
13. Pray 10 Hail Marys and 1 Glory Be to the Father.
14. Pray the Sign of the Cross.

Rosary Pattern

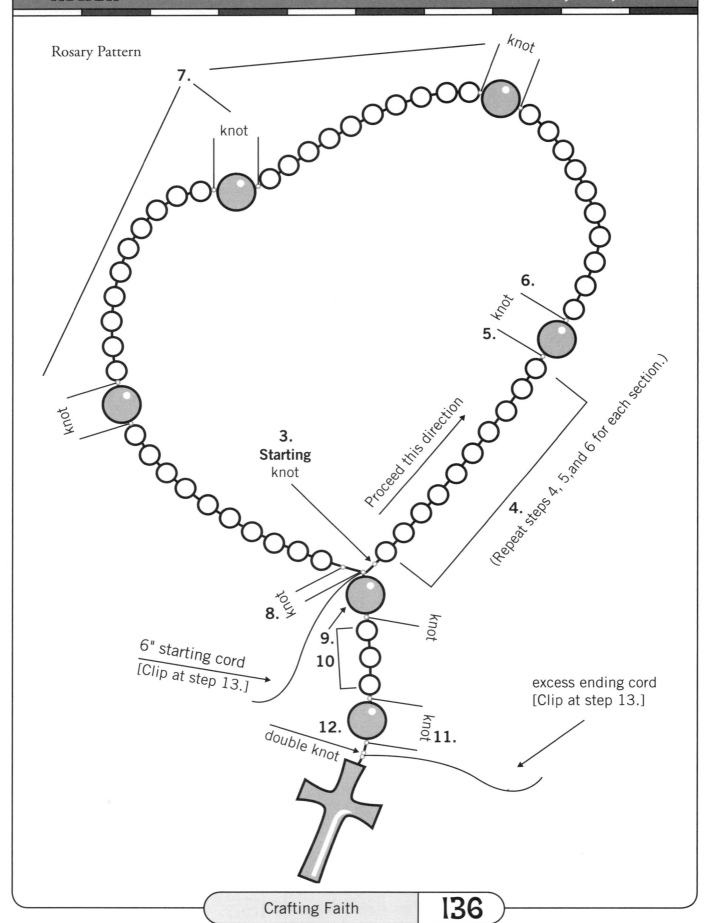

7.

knot

knot

knot

knot

6.

5.

knot

**3.
Starting**
knot

Proceed this direction

4.
(Repeat steps 4, 5, and 6 for each section.)

knot

8. knot

9.
10.

knot

6" starting cord
[Clip at step 13.]

excess ending cord
[Clip at step 13.]

12.
double knot

knot 11.

Rosary Activity Center

Grades 3–8

Materials:

Rosary Bead Kits (to be assembled before the event)

Place the following items in a plastic bag or other container.

53 beads of one color	6 beads of another color
Needle (Optional: Many types of cord are stiff enough to thread beads without a needle, and other cords come with a needlelike wire preattached.)	Toothpick (This is used to make tidy, well-placed knots. Alternatively, you could provide straight-nose beading tweezers.)
3' cord, with a dot marked at 6" from one end	1 crucifix

Note: It is very important that the holes of all 59 beads be the same size and that the cord is the right size for those holes. The beads should fit easily but not loosely, on the cord.

> **FAITH CONNECTION**
> *Make the treasured prayer of the Rosary even more precious by praying it on a rosary that you and your family have made with your own hands and hearts.*

Before You Begin:

Good organization is the key to success in this activity center. Recruit several volunteers well ahead of time. Those with beading or other handiwork experience will be especially valuable for assembling the kits, setting up the work space, and helping participants at the activity center. It will also be vital to have volunteers who pray the Rosary regularly. Their devotion and knowledge will be wonderful assets.

Please encourage the coordinator of this activity center to make a practice rosary well before the event so that he or she can test the instructions and be certain that all materials are suitable.

At the Event:

Set up several work spaces stocked with the following items.

- Rosary Activity Center handout (pages 133–36), 1 for each family
- Clear nail polish or craft glue (for securing knots), one container for every 10 families (Do not use instant adhesives like Superglue or Krazy Glue.)
- Empty egg cartons for sorting beads (optional)

Note: Beads can be a choking hazard for young children. Please remind parents to be vigilant.

Tips for Gathering Materials

Premade Kits: If you are pressed for time, buying premade kits is an option. They are available online and from many Catholic book and religious supply stores. To find them online, type "rosary kits" into a search engine. Prices vary considerably.

Beads: Beads come in a dazzling variety of sizes, shapes, colors, and materials. Because there are so many styles of bead to choose from, you will be able to adapt your purchases to fit the needs and resources of your parish. The most important thing to keep in mind as you select beads is that the holes of all 59 beads should be the same size.

You can purchase your beads online or at a craft or specialty store. If purchasing online, type "beads" or "beading supplies" into search engine. If you are new to beading, you may wish to go to a craft or specialty store to purchase your beads. That way, you can see and compare all the possible varieties of beads, and you will be able to ask advice from the people who work there.

Cord: The most common type of cord available in craft or specialty stores is made of waxed polyester thread. This type of cord is durable and inexpensive but is not available in many colors other than black. If you would like a choice of colors, you may wish to purchase silk cord, which is also sturdy but more expensive than the polyester cord. Whichever type you choose, it should fit cleanly but snugly through the bead.

Silk cord usually comes with a needlelike wire attached to it. The polyester cord usually does not. Before buying polyester or other bulk cord, try threading it through one of the beads you have chosen to see if it will thread through the hole without a needle. If it does not, you may need to provide participants with wires or needles to help them thread their beads.

Crucifix Medals: Most religious supply stores, and even many craft stores, will carry crucifixes and crosses suitable for rosary making. Different stores will call them by different names, so knowing some commonly used terms will help your search considerably. Religious suppliers tend to call them crucifix medals, but other suppliers will call them crucifix charms, rosary crosses, or cross charms.

When searching online (or even when calling local crafts stores), if you run into a dead end using one term, try another and another until you find success. You might also want to search online for premade rosary kits, because many kit suppliers will also sell pieces individually.

Rosary Resources: You may wish to provide some books on praying the Rosary for participants. The following are available from www.LoyolaBooks.org
- *Catholic Prayer for Catholic Families.* Chicago: Loyola Press, 2006.
- Kelly, Liz. *The Rosary: A Path to Prayer.* Chicago: Loyola Press, 2001.
- Odell, Catherine and Margaret Savitkas. *Loyola Kids Book of Everyday Prayer.* Chicago: Loyola Press, 2002.
- Storey, William G. *The Complete Rosary: A Guide to Praying the Mysteries.* Chicago: Loyola Press, 2006.

Note: The missions are often in need of rosaries. Consider asking families to each make one rosary for the missions in addition to their own during the event. Contact a missionary organization (e.g., Catholic Extension Society 800-842-7804 or Divine Word Missionaries 847-272-7600) and arrange to send or deliver rosaries to them. © 2007 Loyola Press. All rights reserved.

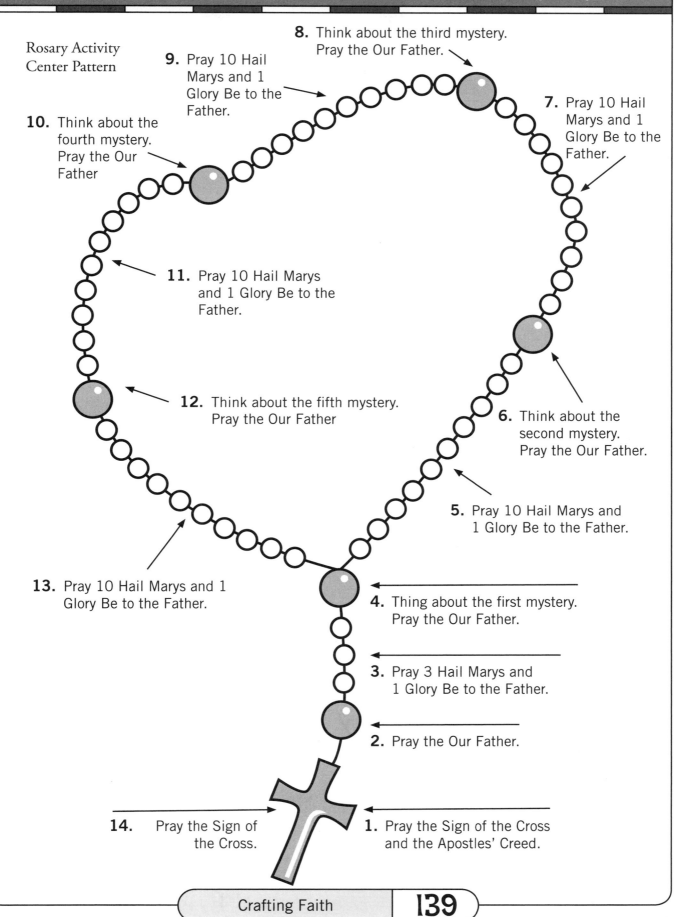

Rosary Activity
Center Pattern

8. Think about the third mystery. Pray the Our Father.

9. Pray 10 Hail Marys and 1 Glory Be to the Father.

7. Pray 10 Hail Marys and 1 Glory Be to the Father.

10. Think about the fourth mystery. Pray the Our Father

11. Pray 10 Hail Marys and 1 Glory Be to the Father.

12. Think about the fifth mystery. Pray the Our Father

6. Think about the second mystery. Pray the Our Father.

5. Pray 10 Hail Marys and 1 Glory Be to the Father.

4. Thing about the first mystery. Pray the Our Father.

13. Pray 10 Hail Marys and 1 Glory Be to the Father.

3. Pray 3 Hail Marys and 1 Glory Be to the Father.

2. Pray the Our Father.

14. Pray the Sign of the Cross.

1. Pray the Sign of the Cross and the Apostles' Creed.

Macramé Rosary

Grades 5–8

Materials:

String (20 ply) or yarn	Diagram of rosary (see page 132)
Wooden cross (approximately 2") with hole in top for string to slide through	Scissors

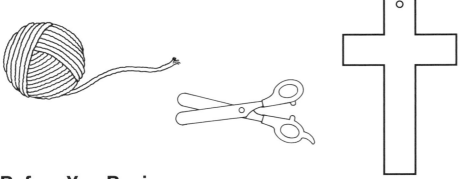

Before You Begin

The length of string needed per student will depend upon the thickness of the string and the ability of the students at making knots close together. Three to five feet of 20-ply string is needed for each rosary. Make a sample rosary to test for length needed and tightness of knots.

Directions:

1. Make ten single knots evenly spaced in a piece of string or yarn for the Hail Marys.

2. Make a double or triple knot for the Our Fathers.

3. Continue around for all five decades. Use a workable length (approximately 18") to knot one decade. Do five lengths, or decades, and double or triple knot them together. This knot becomes the Our Father knot.

4. Attach a piece of string or yarn (approximately 12") to the cross. Make a double or triple knot, space, three single knots, space, and one double or triple knot.

5. Attach this piece to the large part of the rosary in the proper place. (See diagram.)

6. Trim excess string or yarn.

Optional: You may want to make arrangements to have these rosaries blessed.

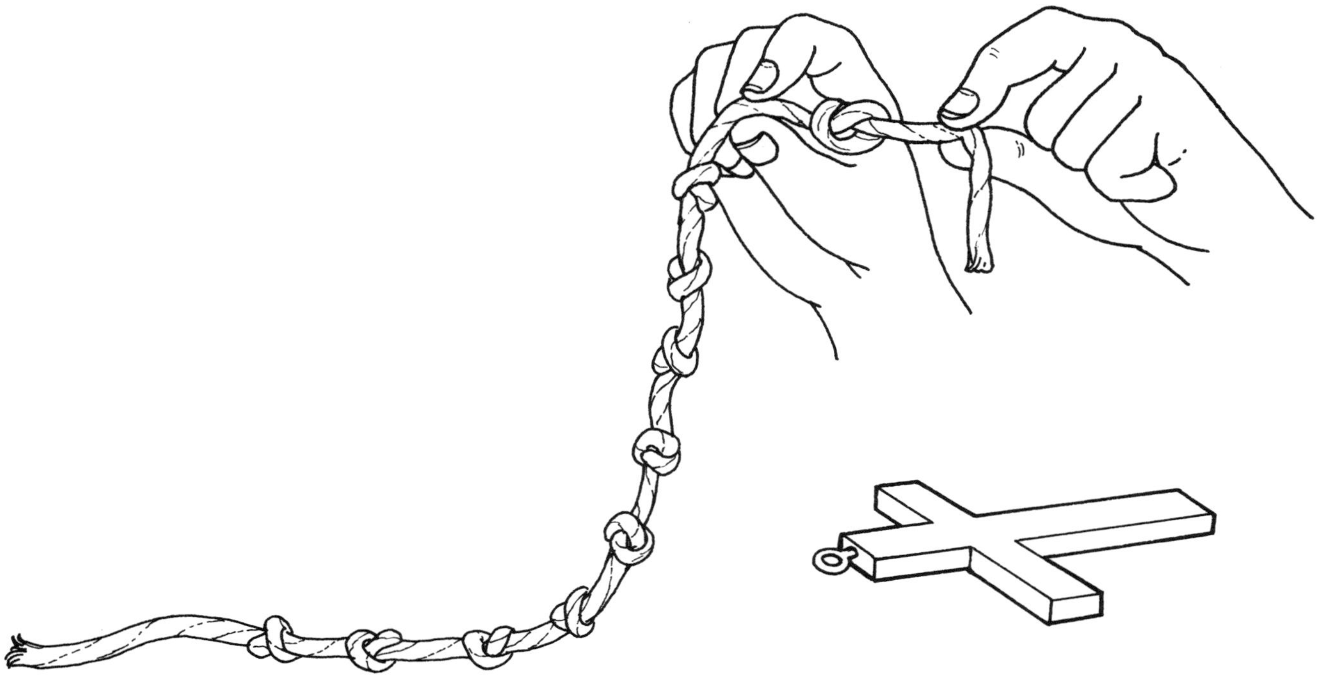

Beatitudes Plaque

Grades 1–4

Materials:

Drawing paper (9" × 12" or 12" × 16")	Glue or stapler
Colored construction paper	Shirts, smocks, or aprons to protect clothing
Crayons, colored chalk, or tempera paint and paintbrushes	Old magazines
Copies of the Beatitudes	Scissors

FAITH CONNECTION

Read the Beatitudes with the children, Matthew 5:1–12. Emphasize that the Beatitudes are Jesus' "recipe" for happiness.

Before Class:

Prepare multiple strips of paper with one beatitude printed on each strip (see Matthew 5:1–12).

Directions:

1. Draw a picture of Jesus sitting on top of a hill. Draw some of his disciples.

2. Cut out magazine pictures of people sharing and helping others. Glue these pictures on the paper with the picture of Jesus you made.

3. Glue or staple one or more of the beatitude strips of paper to your picture.

4. Title your picture if you wish.

5. Glue or staple your picture on a piece of colored construction paper to make a frame.

Beatitudes Banner

Grades 5–8

Materials:

Material for banners: butcher paper or runners from church weddings	Stapler
Pencils	Yarn
Felt-tip pens	Symbol patterns (see page144

FAITH CONNECTION
Read with the children the Beatitudes, Matthew 5:1–12. Emphasize that the Beatitudes are Jesus' "recipe" for happiness. Help the students understand that they can "BE-a-good-ATTITUDE" in the world by following Jesus in his mission of reaching out to others.

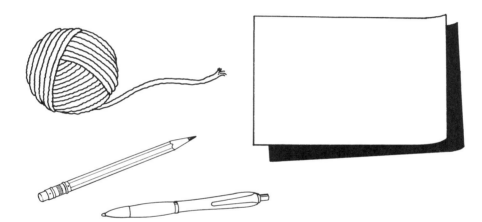

Before Class:

Make copies of suggested symbols. Write the word *Beatitudes* on the chalkboard before class.

Directions:

1. Direct the students to design a simple picture or symbol to represent their chosen beatitude. Use the suggested symbol patterns to help the students with ideas.

2. Write the words of the beatitude on the banner and draw a picture or symbol to illustrate the beatitude.

3. Color the banner with felt-tip pens, using bright, happy colors. The symbol may be outlined in black.

4. Fold the top of the banner down and staple to make a pocket.

5. Slip yarn through the pocket and tie ends together.

Beatitudes Banner Symbols Patterns

Pinecone Shepherd

Grades 1–4

Materials:

Large pinecone, 1 per student	2½" Styrofoam® plastic ball, 1 per student
Glue	Felt or fabric (solid colors)
Chenille stems	"Love One Another" printed on small strips of paper, 1 per student
Small brushes	Optional: Cardboard for stand, sequins, and pins

FAITH CONNECTION

Jesus taught in the two greatest commandments that we are to love God with all our hearts and to love our neighbors as ourselves. Loving our neighbors and ourselves is a way of loving God. These little pinecone shepherds will carry the sign "Love One Another" to remind us how to love.

Before Class:

Prepare a sufficient supply of "Love One Another" signs.

Directions:

1. Glue the Styrofoam® plastic ball to the top of the pinecone.

2. Glue or pin two sequins for the eyes and one for the nose (or use felt).

3. Wrap a chenille stem around the pinecone for arms.

4. Glue a piece of felt or fabric for the headpiece covering.

5. Glue the small "Love One Another" sign between hands.

Optional: The pinecone may be glued to a small piece of cardboard to use as a stand.

 25 minutes

Pinecone Shepherd

Grades 5–8

Materials:

Large pinecone, 1 per student	2½" Styrofoam® plastic ball, 1 per student
Old nylon stockings	Chenille stems
Cotton balls	Pen
Brown or tan thread	White paper
Sequins and pins	Scissors
Scrap felt or fabric (solid colors)	White craft or fabric glue
Thin gold or silver braid or twine	Optional: #32 tie wire

> ### FAITH CONNECTION
> *In John 10:11, Jesus describes himself as the Good Shepherd who has come to lay down his life for the sheep. We are called to love as does Jesus—selflessly.*

Directions:

1. If necessary, carve a small hole in bottom of Styrofoam® plastic ball to have it "sit" properly on pinecone (or break off a few petals of pinecone to make it flat on top). Do not attach ball yet.

2. To make "head" and "nose," work with a partner.
   - Cover entire Styrofoam® plastic ball with a piece of old nylon. Make sure there is enough material to gather for a neck.
   - Add a tiny piece of cotton underneath the nylon to make the nose. Have your partner hold the "head," keeping the nylon tight around the neck while you "pinch" the nose into shape. Tie a piece of thread around the nose to hold the shape.
   - Keeping the nylon tight around the neck, tie another piece of thread around the neck.

3. Glue the head to the top of the pinecone. Wrap more thread around the neck and pinecone to anchor securely.
   (Optional: Attach the head to the cone with #32 tie wire. Wrap wire tightly around ball and cone.)

4. You can make features in the following way.
   - Eyes—Use two sequins and pins.
   - Beard—Fluff out a piece of cotton and glue to chin area.
   - Arms—Wrap a pipe cleaner around the pinecone body.

5. Cut and glue fabric to form headpiece for the shepherd.

6. Tie a piece of gold or silver braid around the forehead.

7. Print "Love One Another" on a small piece of white paper and glue it to the hands of the shepherd.

This Is Your Life: Something Special for a Special Friend

Grades 1–8

FAITH CONNECTION
Jesus taught in the two greatest commandments that we are to love God with all our hearts and to love our neighbors as ourselves. Loving our neighbors and ourselves is a way of loving God.

Materials:

Magazines with colorful pictures	Assorted decorations (colored paper, doilies, lace, stickers, etc.)
Scissors	Poster board
Glue	

Directions:

1. Look through magazines. Cut out anything that reminds you of the person for whom you are making this gift. If the person loves music, look for pictures with a musical theme. For sports, use basketball, soccer, skating, or whichever sport your friend likes best. Consider favorite foods and hobbies. Use pictures, words, or a short story or poem about your friend.

2. Arrange the items attractively before you glue them onto the poster board. Decorate with lace, colored stars, etc. Try to show how special your friend is using pictures.

Living Stones

Grades 1–8

Materials:

Stones (paperweight size), smooth and clean, any shape, 1 per student	Poster, gouache, or acrylic paints
Brushes	Newspapers
Shirts, smocks, or aprons to protect clothing	Optional: Felt and glue

Before Class:

Wash stones and let them dry so there is a clean surface on which to paint. Make sure the stone has at least one smooth surface.

Directions:

1. Have the students study their rocks and find the best place to paint their names.

2. Let the students' creativity and imagination flow as they paint and decorate their personal "name stones."

3. Optional: Glue felt to the bottom of the stone.

4. Let the students look up their patron saints and read about them while the rocks are drying. Grades 1 and 2: While they are painting, tell the students personally about their patron saints.

FAITH CONNECTION

St. Peter wrote about Jesus in the Bible as the "living stone" who was rejected by the people in power but approved and precious in God's eyes. We, too, are "living stones" (1 Peter 2:4–5). We are God's building stones of the Church, with Jesus as the cornerstone. God wants to build Church with you and me. Let the stones with our names on them remind us of all the saints who have lived before us. We, too, should strive to become good and loving persons.

If possible, obtain a copy of Butler's Lives of the Saints *or some other book on saints. Have the students read about the saints after whom they were named. Children are delighted to find out about their patron saints. This will help make the rock project more meaningful for the students. You may wish to put the Scripture verse 1 Peter 2:4–5 on the chalkboard.*

Saint Clip Activity Center

Grades 5–8

Materials:

Beading wire	Crimp beads, 2 per student
Saint medals, 1 per student	Clasps, 1 per student
Beads, 3 per student	Needle nose or beading pliers
Wire cutters	

Directions:

1. Slide one crimp bead onto the beading wire. (See page 151 for illustrations of the directions.)

2. Thread your chosen saint medal onto the wire.

3. Loop the end of the wire back through the crimp bead, leaving a half-inch to quarter-inch tail.

4. Tighten the wire loop, pushing the crimp bead close to the saint medal.

5. Using pliers, flatten the crimp bead, securing the wires in place.

6. Thread three beads onto the wire. You can cover the "tail" wire by threading that through the bead along with the main wire.

7. Thread another crimp bead onto the wire. Be careful if the beads you are using have holes larger than the crimp bead. It could slide into a bead and get stuck.

8. Thread a clasp onto the wire.

9. Loop the end of the wire back through the crimp bead.

10. Tighten the loop, pulling the end of the wire to bring the clasp, the crimp bead, and the three other beads close together. You will want a little bit of slack.

11. When everything is in position, use pliers to flatten the crimp bead.

12. Use wire cutters to snip the excess wire to leave a quarter-inch tail. Tuck the tail into the beads.

> **FAITH CONNECTION**
>
> *Through the Communion of Saints, we are connected with the saints in heaven and they are present to us, helping and supporting us. Make a saint clip with a medal honoring your favorite saint. Clip it to your jacket or backpack as a reminder that, wherever you go, you have a companion on the journey.*

Saint Clip Activity Center Directions

1.

2.

3.

4.

5.

6.

7.

8.

9.

10.

11.

12.

Stick Puppets

Grades 1–4

Materials:

Catalogs	Glue or paste
Greeting cards	Cardboard
Magazines	Popsicle sticks
Scissors	

Directions:

1. Cut pictures out of old cards, catalogs, magazines, etc.

2. Paste each picture on cardboard. Trim the cardboard to the shape of the picture. Make a long handle out of the cardboard or use a popsicle stick. Leave other parts of the picture for scenery around your picture. For example, leave a tree in the background in a picture where a boy is throwing a ball.

Box Puppets

Grades 1–4

Materials:

Small boxes (such as individual serving cereal boxes), 1 per student	Construction paper
Scissors	Fabric scraps
Glue	Yarn

These puppets can be used with the activity on page 152.

FAITH CONNECTION

Point out that the Ten Commandments are God's Laws. As they did with the stick puppets (see page 152), have the students present a skit with the box puppets to show how rules are a part of their life.

Before Class:

Score the box in the middle of the front side and cut down both sides. Leave the back in one piece. Fold the box in half.

Directions:

1. Cover the box with construction paper.

2. Create a face on the box using construction paper, fabric scraps, yarn, etc.

3. Put your thumb in the bottom of the box and your fingers in the top to make the puppet move.

25 minutes

Sock Puppets

Grades 1–8

Materials:

Odds and ends of rickrack, yarn, cotton, felt, fabric, etc.	Glue or needle and thread
Buttons	Scissors
Socks, 1 per student	

These puppets can be used with the activity on page 152.

These puppets can be used with the activity on page 152.

> ### FAITH CONNECTION
> *Point out that the Ten Commandments are God's Laws. As with the stick puppets (see page 152), have the students present a skit with the sock puppets to show how rules are a part of their life.*

Directions:

1. Glue or sew on the mouth, eyes, etc.
2. Add hair and ears.

Paper Bag Puppets

Grades 1–8

Materials:

Paper bag (small lunch bag size), 1 per student	Odds and ends of rickrack, yarn, cotton, felt, fabric, buttons, etc.
Buttons	Scissors
Glue	

These puppets can be used with the activity on page 152.

> ### FAITH CONNECTION
> *Point out that the Ten Commandments are God's Laws. As with the stick puppets (see page 152), have the students present a skit with the paper bag puppets to show how rules are a part of their life.*

Directions:

1. Draw a face on the bottom flap of the paper bag or glue on odds and ends to make a face on the flap.

2. Add yarn or fabric for hair, cap, ears, etc. on your puppet.

Let Your Light Shine Paper Candles

Grades 1–4

Materials:

Cardboard tubes (such as toilet paper rolls, or paper towel rolls), 1 per student	Scripture verses (e.g., "You are the light of the world," Matthew 5:14, "Let your light shine," adapted from Matthew 5:16)
Aluminum foil	Glue or tape
Tissue paper in red, yellow, orange colors	Optional: Cardboard or poster board

> **FAITH CONNECTION**
> *Read aloud with the children Matthew 5:14–16, "You are the light of the world. Your light must shine before others." Invite them to complete a project that reminds them to let their light shine for others.*

You are the light of the world.
Matthew 5:14

Before Class:

Prepare Scripture verses on the symbolism of light.

Directions:

1. Cover the tube with aluminum foil and tape or glue foil in place.

2. Insert tissue paper in the top of the tube to resemble a flame. Glue or tape tissue into place if necessary.

3. Glue or tape a Scripture verse to the candle.

Optional: Glue or tape the candle to a round piece of cardboard or poster board to make a base for the candle to stand. The cardboard should be cut 2" to 3" larger than the tube.

Get Ready for Jesus: A Lamp

Grades 1–8

Materials:

Paper plate, 1 per student	Crayons or markers
Scissors	Red tissue paper
Pencil	Tape or glue

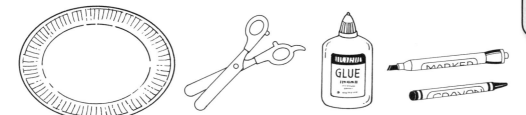

> **FAITH CONNECTION**
> *Read aloud with the children the Parable of the Ten Virgins (Matthew 25:1–13). Explain that Jesus is encouraging us always to be ready to love and serve others.*

Directions:

1. Cut the paper plate in half. Save the extra half for another project.
2. Cut a handle out of one side of the paper plate.
3. Write "I Am Ready" on the lamp. Decorate the lamp as desired.
4. Cut flame shapes from red tissue paper and crinkle them.
5. Tape or glue the flame shapes onto the top of the lamp.
6. Display the lamp as a reminder that your faith in Jesus makes you ready for him to come again.

Suggestions:

1. Cut the red flame out of red construction paper.
2. Cover a cardboard flame with tin foil and glue it on the lamp.
3. Color the lamp on a whole paper plate.
4. Use a colored paper plate for the lamp.
5. Omit the handle and make a temple lamp to use with the story of Samuel (1 Samuel 3).
6. Write "Let Your Light Shine" on the lamp. Tell of ways you can show God's love to others.
7. Use the lamp to illustrate the songs "This Little Gospel Light of Mine" and "Give Me Oil in My Lamp."

I Am Ready

Monograms

Grades 5–8

Materials:

Paper	Corkwood
Cloth	Scissors
Felt	Needle and thread or glue
Chenille Stems	Paper
Lace	Pencils

> **FAITH CONNECTION**
> *We use signs and symbols to express ourselves. Invite the children to do a project in which they will create symbols—monograms—of what they have learned this year.*

Directions:

1. Monograms can be used on such things as clothing, luggage, or shoes. Shapes, kinds of letters, and size can vary greatly for monograms. Some suggestions are illustrated. Some monograms are easier to cut with a razor blade than with scissors. Monograms must be designed to fit into a specific size or shape. Students will create the size and shape of their own monograms. Monograms shaped from chenille stems are tacked into place with a needle and thread. They must be removed before laundering or they will rust. Other monograms can be sewed or glued, depending on the materials used.

2. Have the students think about what they have learned this year. Have them design their monogram to symbolize one particular idea. Some ideas are saints, friendship, gifts and talents, and prayer.

3. This can be a two-session project. The first session would give students time to get their thoughts down on paper and design a realistic monogram. The second session would be for the students to actually create their monograms.

Shoe Box Scene

Grades 3–8

Materials:

Newspapers	Scissors or knife
Shoe box and lid	Tissue paper or cellophane
Paint and paintbrushes	Odds and ends for scene (i.e., twigs, aluminum foil, matches, sponge, thread)

You may want to have aides for the younger students.

> ### FAITH CONNECTION
> *Discuss with the students how the Church is called to be the spiritual guide to the world. Using this theme, have the students create a shoebox scene. They could depict what the Christian's responsibility is to other people: family members, minorities, refugees, immigrants, the poor, the Church, the local community, and the world.*

Directions:

1. Cut a small hole in one end of the box with a scissors or a knife. Cut a round or oblong hole in the lid at one end.

2. With the lid off, paint a scene on the bottom of the box. Keep checking back through the hole in the end of the box to see the scene that appears.

3. Put the lid on to see whether the hole is letting in enough light. The hole in the lid needs to be at the end opposite the peephole.

Note: Ask students to bring their own boxes and other items for their scenes. Prepare a list in advance and send it home to the parents.

Various things can be used for the scene. Use crumpled paper for a rough sea, a ship with matches for masts, a matchbox house with a piece of mirror for a lake or aluminum foil for water. Bits of sponge on a twig can be a tree.

The light in the box will change depending upon whether tissue paper or cellophane is used over the hole in the lid. Cellophane is best if you have it. Thread can be used to hang such things as birds or airplanes from the lid.

Crayon T-shirt Transfer

Grades 1–8

Materials:

Crayons	T-shirts, 1 per child
Sandpaper	Iron

FAITH CONNECTION

As with the Shoebox Scene (see page 160), have the students create Crayon T-shirt Transfers, depicting what the Christian's responsibility is to other people: family members, minorities, refugees, immigrants, the poor, the Church, the local community, and the world.

Directions:

1. Invite the students to draw a design on bumpy pieces of sandpaper. Make sure they press hard.

2. Turn the drawn side of the sandpaper face down on a T-shirt and place a cloth on top of the paper

3. Run a hot, dry iron over the cloth and sandpaper for a minute or so, then remove the sandpaper to reveal their custom T-shirts.

Rainbow Picture 1

Grades 1–4

Materials:

Blue finger paint (see recipe below)	Construction paper of various colors
White paper (about 12" × 18")	Rainbow stripe pattern
Sponge	Glue
Water	Scissors
Newspapers	

FAITH CONNECTION
Read aloud with the children Genesis 9:11–17 and point out how the rainbow is a reminder to us of the covenant that God established with the human family.

Directions:

1. Cover table with newspapers. Put a white sheet of paper on the table and dampen the sheet with a sponge and water. Put about a tablespoon of finger paint on the paper and cover the entire paper with the paint. Make swirling motions.

2. While the paint is drying, wash the students' hands. Have the students make rainbows from construction paper, using various colors for the stripes of the rainbow.

3. Cut out the rainbow stripes.

4. Glue the rainbow stripes to the finger-painted background when it is dry.

Finger Paint Recipe:
Mix 3 tbs. of sugar with 1/2 tsp. cornstarch. Add 2 c. cold water and cook over low flame. Stir constantly. Divide mixture into four or five portions and add different food coloring or poster paint to each portion.

Rainbow Picture 2

Grades 1–4

Materials:

Newspapers	White paper or newsprint
Paint and brushes or crayons	Materials for cleaning up

Directions:

1. Pass out paper to each student. Remind the students that the rainbow is a symbol of a covenant and God's presence with the people.

2. Have the students draw their own rainbow picture using paints or crayons.

Scroll

Grades 1–8

Materials:

White shelf paper	Two twigs 4" longer than the width of the shelf paper
Black crayons	Ribbon
Glue	

You will need teacher aides for the younger students.

Directions:

1. Have the students think about a promise, or "covenant," they would make with a friend.

2. Have the students print their promises in the center of the shelf paper. (Grades 1 and 2 will need help with the printing.)

3. Glue a twig to each end of the paper.

4. Glue ribbon to the ends and tie scroll.

5. Have the students share their covenant with their friends.

Stained Glass Mobiles

Grades 3–8

FAITH CONNECTION
Read or summarize the story of Joseph, the son of Jacob, from Genesis 37–50.

Materials:

Cardboard	Newspapers
Aluminum foil	Glass stain paint
Colored tissue paper	Cord
Scissors	Heavy wire or clothes hangers
Pencils	Mobile patterns (see page 166)

Before Class:

Make ample patterns for the students to use.

Directions:

1. Cover the tables with newspapers.

2. Create pieces for the mobile by tracing shapes on the cardboard using the patterns provided (harp, crown, trumpet, Joseph's coat, shepherd's crook, and tablets). Use foil, tissue paper, patterns, and glass stain paint to make the mobile pieces. Older students can to make their mobile pieces more elaborate by cutting out the center and adding colored tissue paper inlays or otherwise decorating the pieces.

3. Attach cords to each piece and attach to a wire or clothes hanger. Try various lengths until you have the right balance for each element on the mobile.

Stained Glass Mobiles Patterns

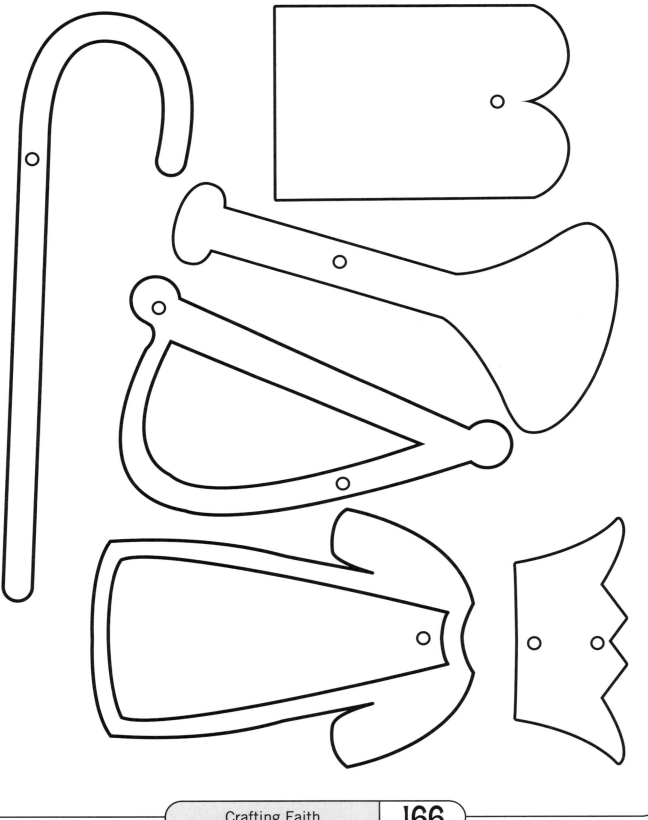

Sandpaper Desert Painting

Grades 1–4

Materials:

Crayons	Sandpaper, large enough to draw on, 1 piece per student
Optional: Iron and drawing paper	

FAITH CONNECTION

This "sand painting" project will remind us of how Moses led the Israelites through the desert in search of the promised land of freedom and abundance. This journey of the Israelites is meaningful in our Christian experience today because we view our life as a journey towards God and God's promises.

Directions:

1. Ask the students whether they have ever been to a desert. What was it like? Try to get the students to "feel" and create the mood of a desert scene: hot and dry. To create the sense of heat, dryness, and thirst, have the students use a lot of "warm" or "hot" colors such as orange, red, and yellow in their paintings.

2. Have the students draw their desert pictures directly on the sandpaper.

3. Press crayons hard in some areas, lightly in others. The students will have a bright, rough-textured drawing.

Optional: To make a print of their drawing, have the students place their drawing crayon-side down on a piece of drawing paper. Iron the back side of the sandpaper with a hot iron. Pull the sandpaper and drawing paper apart. Now you have two drawings!

 25 minutes

Burning Bush Banner

Grades 1–8

Materials:

8" × 10" poster board or construction paper piece, 1 per student	Felt pieces in browns, golds, oranges, yellows, reds
Glue	Scissors
Yarn	Patterns (see page 169)
Pencils	

Before Class:

Cut out the burning bush pieces for grades 1–3 so that the students only have to arrange and glue the colored "burning bush" pieces on the poster board or construction paper.

Directions:

1. Pass out patterns and let the students trace them onto the colored felt.

2. Cut the felt pieces and arrange them on the poster board or construction paper so that they form a burning bush. Glue the pieces in place.

3. Fringe the edges of the poster board or construction paper by making small cuts with scissors every ¼" to ½".

4. To make a picture, glue yarn to the top of the poster board or construction paper. Tie yarn together to form loop and hang.

Burning Bush Banner Patterns

Sand Art

Grades 4–8

Materials:

Construction paper	Sand
Glue	

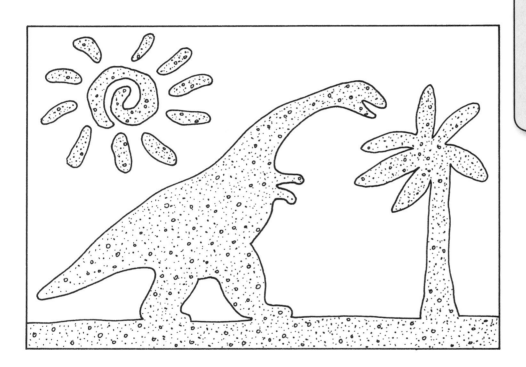

> **FAITH CONNECTION**
>
> *Sand art is an interesting way of using part of God's creation to express oneself. Also called sand painting, this is a simple but satisfying craft that is good for Earth Day in the springtime or any dry summer day that follows.*

Directions:

1. Give students each a piece of construction paper and allow them to draw a picture or write words with the glue. *Make sure that they do not put globs of glue in any one spot.*

2. Before the glue dries, use your hand to pour dry sand onto the glue.

3. Let the paper sit for a few minutes and then shake off the excess sand.

4. Let the picture dry flat for a half hour or more, depending on how much glue was used.

Note: This activity can also be done with colored sand, but, for projects on a budget, regular sand works just as well.

 20 minutes

Tau Cross

Grades 1–2

Materials:

Construction paper, black or dark color	Scissors
White glue	Tau Cross pattern (see page 172)

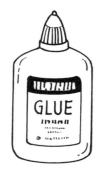

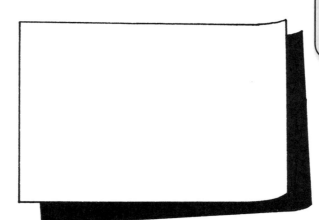

Before Class:

On white paper, draw the Tau Cross for each student.

Directions:

1. Help the students cut out the Tau Cross you have copied.

2. Glue the white Tau Cross to the darker piece of construction paper

3. Pray the prayer Glory Be to the Father together and talk about the blessings God has given each one.

Tau Cross Pattern

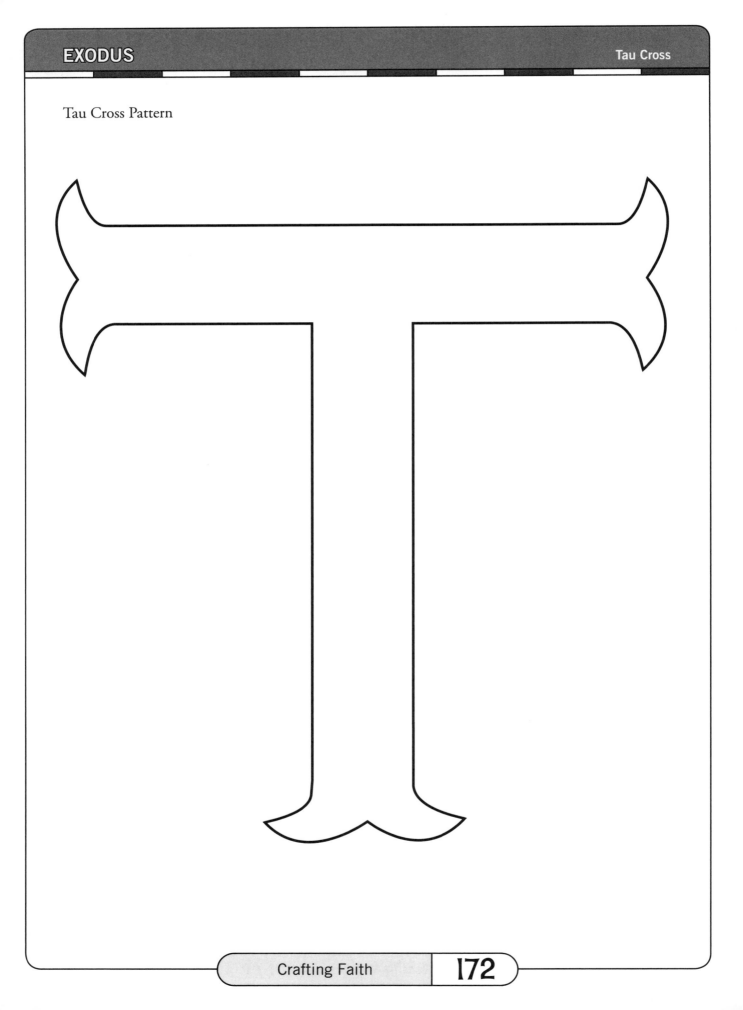

 20 minutes

Ten Commandments Clay Tablets

Grades 1–4

Materials:

Newspapers or other table covering	2 cups flour
Pencils	1 cup water
Recipe for Clay:	Clay or play dough (see recipe below)
1 cup salt	

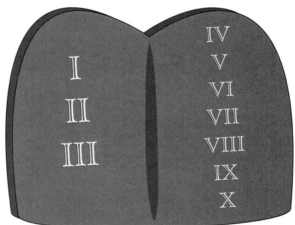

> **FAITH CONNECTION**
> *Remind the children that when Moses came down from Mount Sinai, he was holding stone tablets on which were inscribed the Ten Commandments (see Exodus 31:18).*

Before You Begin:

1. Make play dough using the following ingredients: 1 cup salt, 2 cups flour, 1 cup water.
2. Mix salt and flour.
3. Add water gradually and mix with hands.
4. Form in balls and seal in a tightly covered container.

Directions:

1. Soften clay or play dough.
2. Divide in half.
3. Make a tablet as shown in the picture. Flatten the dough and push it into shape.
4. Use a pencil on the clay tablets. Write the Roman numerals to represent the Ten Commandments.
5. Place the tablets on a shelf to dry for 24 hours before the students take the tablets home.

 30 minutes

Eye of God Mexican Yarn Ornament (*Ojo de Dios*)

Grades 3–8

Materials:

Two 12" craft sticks or sticks about 1" thick (twigs, popsicle sticks, toothpicks)	6" piece of cardboard, 1 per student
Scissors	Optional: Glue
Various balls of yarn in four colors (length depends upon how large you wish the god's eye to be)	

You will need aides to help the younger students.

Directions:

1. Glue the sticks together or wrap the yarn around both sticks at right angles with centers matching to secure them in the shape of a cross.

2. Tie the end of one color of yarn around the sticks at their centers so that the knot is in the back. Always work with the front side facing you.

3. Hold the crossed sticks in one hand and the yarn in the other. Turn the cross frame and weave the yarn in a circular manner, wrapping it completely around each stick as you come to it.

4. You may change colors at any time. Tuck the old and new yarn ends under and continue wrapping the new color.

5. Continue wrapping yarn to within three-fourths inch of the stick ends.

6. Trim off excess yarn and knot or tuck yarn end under.

7. Add pompoms to the ends of the sticks if desired. To make pompoms, loop yarn around your thumb and first finger, tie the loop in the center and then cut through the ends.

FAITH CONNECTION

The Ojo de Dios, literally translated from the Spanish, means "eye of god" and was a symbol used by the indigenous people of northwestern Mexico. This design has also been found as far south as Peru and as far east as Egypt.

Although the indigenous people did not know God as Jesus, they did know there was a "Great Spirit" greater than themselves. They felt a need for prayer and used this symbol as a request for health and protection.

We can use this as a Christian symbol today by observing that the center is a cross and by reflecting on the power of the cross and Jesus' Resurrection as a sign of God's love for all. The four beams of the cross reach to the four ends of the earth: north, south, east, and west.

 20 minutes

Jeremiah Pinch Pots

Grades 1–8

Materials:

Old shirts	Water
Clay	Plastic
Sponge	Sharp pencil or round toothpick

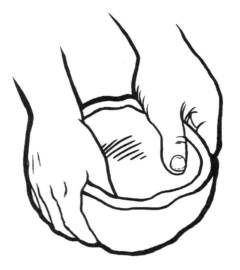

FAITH CONNECTION

Jeremiah was a prophet who was sent by God to watch a potter at his wheel. God then told Jeremiah, "Like clay in the hand of the potter, so are you in my hand" (Jeremiah 18:1–6).

Tips about Clay:

1. There are many different kinds of clay. Some clays are self-hardening, others are water based and can be baked in a regular oven. Whichever kind you choose, keep clay in plastic containers until ready to use.

2. Knead clay with hands until soft before beginning. Then proceed with the project.

Directions:

1. Use a piece of plastic to protect the work table and to prevent the clay from sticking to the table.

2. Break clay into pieces about the size of a tennis ball and roll until completely smooth.

3. Hold ball of clay loosely in the palm of your hand and begin to push the thumb of the other hand down into the center of the ball.

4. With the thumb on the inside and the fingers on the outside, gently squeeze the clay. Hold the clay slightly sideways and rotate slowly.

5. Work upward from the bottom of the ball, squeezing and pinching in a continuous spiraling movement until the walls of the pot are ¼" thick.

6. To work the neck or upper part of the walls, reverse the position of the thumb and fingers and gently squeeze the rim until it is round and even.

7. Smooth out any cracks. If the pot is too dry, dampen it with a wet sponge.

8. Have each student "carve" his or her first name or initials on the bottom of the pot. Use a sharp pencil or a round toothpick for this.

9. Let the clay pots sit on a shelf for 24 hours before letting the students take them home.

🕐 20 minutes

Crowns

Grades 1–2

Materials:

Construction Paper	Scissors
Patterns (see page 178)	White glue
Glitter	Stapler
Sequins	

You will need aides for this project.

Directions:

1. Cut crowns out of construction paper following the patterns provided on page 178.

2. Each student may decorate his or her crown with glitter and sequins.

3. Fit the crown to each student's head. Staple the crown together in the back.

Crowns Patterns

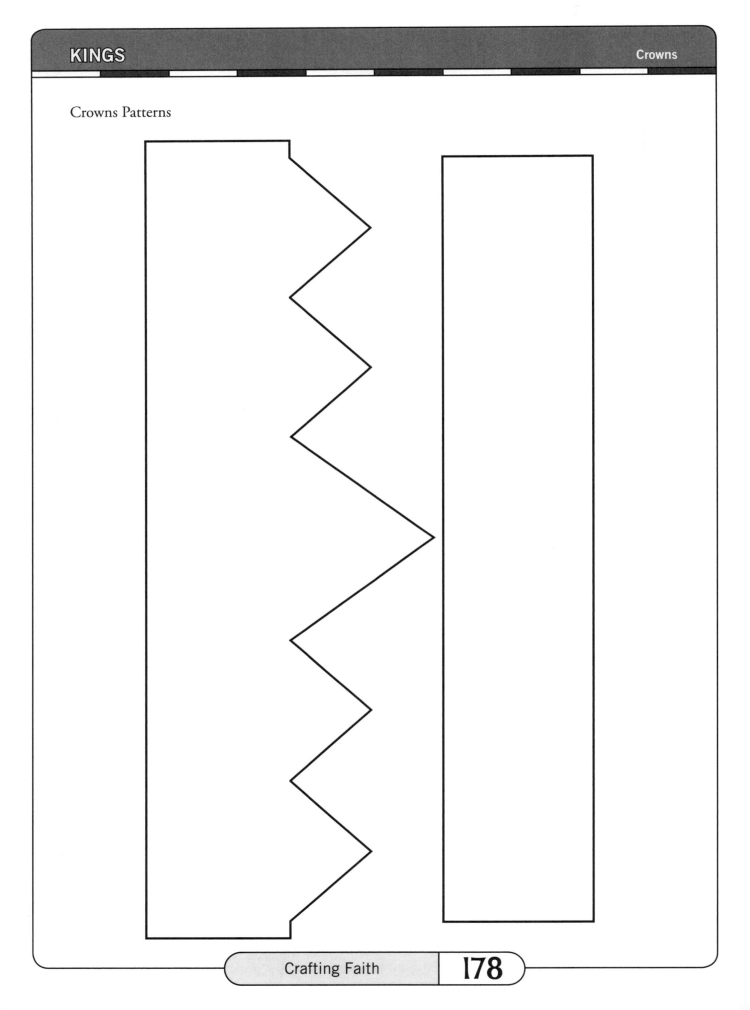

 30 minutes

Seed Plaque

Grades 3–8

Materials:

Pattern (see page 180)	Pencils
Poster board	Popsicle sticks
Glue	Various kinds of seeds and grains such as rice, birdseed, flower seeds, orange seeds, or grapefruit seeds

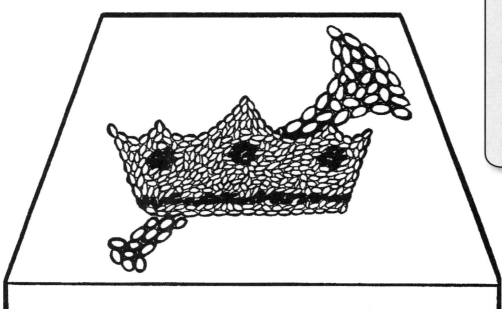

FAITH CONNECTION

The symbols of the crown and trumpet suggested here come from an understanding of the prophets' mission. The prophets were spokespersons for God in their own society reminding the leaders and people of God's Word and the duty of justice for all. Crowns are symbolic of kingship and trumpets are symbolic of the voice of the prophets.

Directions:

1. Trace the pattern of the crown and trumpet from page 180 onto a piece of poster board.

2. Cover a small space of the picture with glue and fill it with seeds or grains. Repeat using various colors until the pattern is complete. Try not to fill an entire shape with a single color. Use a family of colors that are close in hue, such as green with chartreuse; light, dark, bright, and dull shades of blue; and red, maroon, and pink. Work with popsicle sticks to help keep the various colors in line.

Seed Plaque Pattern

Christmas Mural

Grades 1–3

Materials:

Plain shelf paper or wrapping paper	Glue
Christmas cards	Crayons or magic markers
Scissors	

FAITH CONNECTION
Remind the children that at Christmas we celebrate the birth of Jesus the Son of God.

Merry Christmas

Directions:

1. Cut out pictures from Christmas cards.

2. On the strip of shelf paper, glue the pictures to show the sequence of events of the Nativity.

3. Decorate the mural with crayons or magic markers.

4. Hang the mural on the wall.

Ribbon Greeting Cards

Grades 1–8

Materials:

Colored construction paper	Glue
Shiny ribbon	Patterns (see page 183)
Scissors	

You may wish to have aides for the younger students.

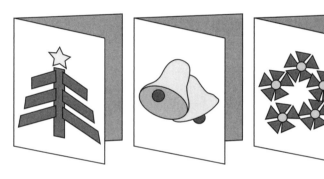

Directions:

1. Fold the construction paper in half.

2. Plan a simple design on the front of the card using the patterns on page 183. Fill in the design with strips of ribbon. The strips will vary in length depending upon the design chosen.

3. For a Christmas tree, cut 6 pieces of green ribbon. Cut the ribbon into 3 different sizes, each a bit longer than the others. Cut 2 pieces in each size, shorter for the top and longer for the bottom. Cut a star and tree trunk from gold ribbon. Glue in place. Glue the pieces of green ribbon to the construction paper in the shape of a tree. Open the card and write a greeting.

4. For a holly wreath, cut 25 small triangles from green ribbon and glue to construction paper to form a wreath. Cut 12 circles from red ribbon for the berries. Glue these onto the wreath. Make a bow with gold ribbon and glue it to the bottom of the wreath.

5. For bells, draw 2 bell shapes from the pattern. On construction paper, glue four strips of ribbon about 1/8" apart on each bell shape. When the glue is dry, cut out and glue the bells to the Christmas card. Cut 2 small circles from another piece of ribbon and glue them in place for bell clappers. Fold a length of ribbon and glue it to the tops of the bells.

Note: For grades 1 and 2, precut ribbons in the shape of the patterns provided.

Ribbon Greeting Cards Patterns

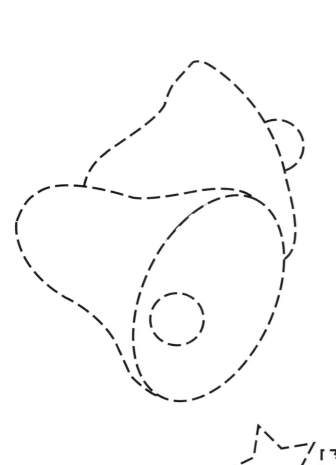

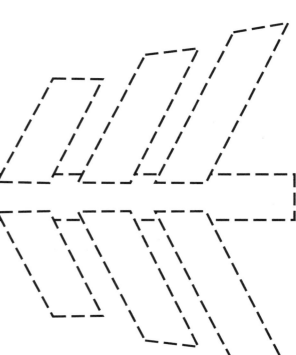

Candle Glow

Grades 1–8

Materials:

5½" × 6" deep lilac construction paper, 1 per student	Deep blue, red, silver, and gold foil papers or tissue paper
Paste or glue	Pencil
Scissors	Patterns (see page 185)

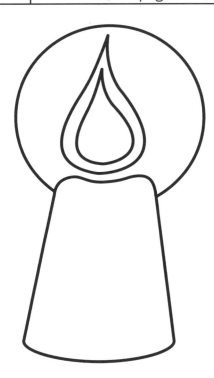

FAITH CONNECTION
Read aloud to the children John 1:1–9 and point out that the "true light" that John speaks of is Jesus. Invite the children to make a project in which they represent Jesus as the true light who has come into the world to dispel the darkness.

Before Class:

Have ample pattern pieces cut out. Decide how much of the foil covering or tissue paper you want to have prepared in advance for younger students.

Directions:

1. Fold the construction paper to measure 5½" × 3". Trace the patterns of the candle and flame from the design on page 185 onto foil papers or tissue paper and cut them out. Make the candle blue, the inner flame silver, the middle flame red, the outer circle gold.

2. Glue the gold circle to the construction paper equidistant from the top and side edges. Glue the red flame on top, positioning it as in the illustration above, putting the silver flame on top of the red flame.

3. Glue the candle into position, overlapping the lower edge of the gold circle.

Candle Glow Patterns

Pinecone Angel

Grades 1–8

Materials:

2½" Styrofoam® plastic ball, 1 per student	Large pinecone, 1 per student
Foil	Felt
Glue	Chenille stems
Sequins or glitter	Golf tee, 1 per student
Yarn	

You will need aides for the younger students.

> **FAITH CONNECTION**
>
> *Remind the children that in the story of Jesus' birth in the Gospel of Luke, we learn that angels proclaimed the birth of Jesus and sang his praise. Point out that we call these angels* heralds, *which means they are messengers of God. Invite the students to create a craft that represents the herald angels of Christmas.*

Before Class:

Have pieces cut and ready to glue for grades 1 and 2.

Directions:

1. Glue Styrofoam® plastic ball to the top end of the pinecone.

2. Cut wings from foil. Insert and glue wings between the scales of the pinecone.

3. Add features made from sequins, yarn, and felt. Form and glue on chenille stems for the arms and halo. Glue on another chenille stem to make a stand.

4. Add a golf tee for the trumpet.

Optional: Angel Ornament—Assemble an angel as above but add a hanger at the top of the head with fine string or wire. Apply a strip of glue to each wing and add glitter.

 20 minutes

Christmas Symbols

Grades 1–8

Materials:

Black construction paper	Pattern pieces (see page 188–89)
White construction paper	Pencils
Scissors	Glue

This project can be used for all levels, depending upon the complexity of the symbol chosen in the patterns. Grades 1 and 2 may want to use single-piece patterns.

FAITH CONNECTION
Remind the children that as Catholics, we use many signs and symbols to express our faith. Invite the children to create symbols that express our joy over the birth of Jesus.

Directions:

1. Using the candle, angel, bell, Christmas tree, or dove pattern, have the students trace around their chosen pattern piece on either black or white construction paper.

2. After each piece of the pattern is cut out, apply it with glue to a piece of construction paper. If students trace on the black, they would glue the pieces onto a white piece of construction paper. If they trace on white, they would glue the white pieces onto the black construction paper. This will create a positive/negative effect.

3. Older students could be instructed to cut their designs into pieces to give a stained-glass effect to the finished product.

Christmas Symbols Patterns

Christmas Symbols Patterns

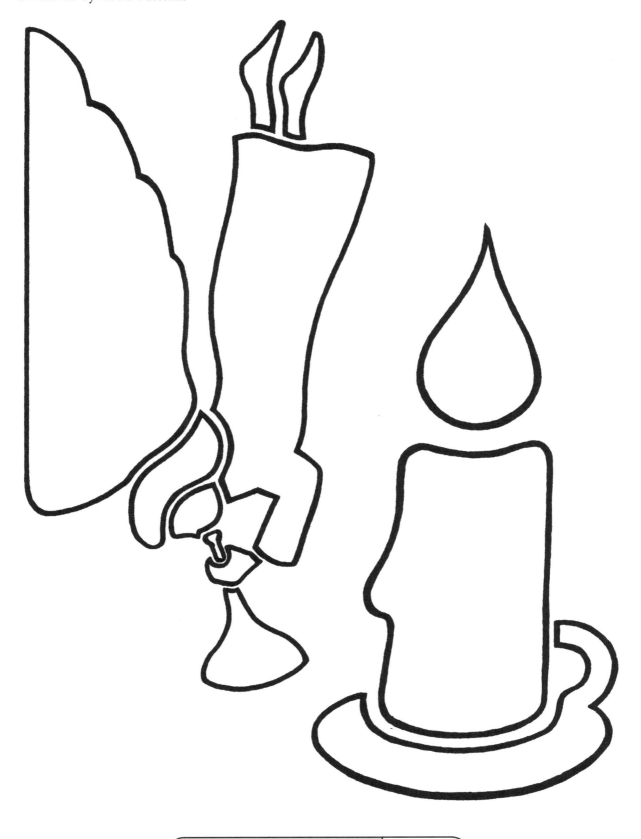

Silhouettes

Grades 3–8

Materials:

Black construction paper	Cardboard (same size as white paper)
White construction paper	Bright lamp
Sharp pencil	Ribbon or heavy yarn
Scissors	Cellophane tape
Assorted colored paper	Glue

FAITH CONNECTION

The Book of Genesis tells us that we are created in the image and likeness of God. This activity allows the children to focus on an image of themselves and to remember that they are made in God's likeness.

Directions:

1. Stand or sit between a bright light and a blank wall. Stand sideways so the shadow of your profile falls on the wall. Use the bright lamp to get a strong shadow.

2. Tape a sheet of black construction paper against the wall so your shadow falls on the black paper. The shadow is your silhouette.

3. Ask a friend to trace your silhouette on the paper. Remember to stand or sit still!

4. Carefully cut out the silhouette and set it aside.

5. Glue a sheet of white paper to the cardboard. Place the silhouette in the center and glue it in place.

6. Decorate the border on the white paper as you wish. Tape a ribbon or heavy yarn to the back of the silhouette in order to hang it.

Note: This can be a Christmas, Valentine's Day, or Mother's Day gift.

Christmas Shadow Pictures

Grades 1–8

Materials:

9" aluminum pie pan	Scissors
Black felt	Hanger
Black rickrack or trim	Silhouette patterns (see page 192)
Glue	

You may need aides with this project to either help younger children cut out the silhouettes or to precut the silhouettes.

FAITH CONNECTION
As a group, brainstorm all of the characters in the stories of the Nativity from the Gospels of Matthew and Luke. List them on the board. Tell the children that they will create shadow pictures of some of these characters and scenes from the Nativity story.

Directions:

1. Using a pattern provided on page 192, cut the Christmas silhouette and star out of black felt.
2. Glue the scene onto the inside of the pie pan, positioning the star above the figure.
3. Glue rickrack around the edge of the pan for the frame.
4. Glue a hanger on the back of the pie pan.

Christmas Shadow Pictures Patterns

Christmas Angel

Grades 1–8

Materials:

Thin cardboard 5" long and 4" high for a cylinder 1½" in diameter (or use an empty toilet tissue roll), 1 per student	White and peach felt pieces
Stapler	Needle and thread
Thin cardboard for wings and halo	1¾" Styrofoam® plastic balls, 1 per student
Brown felt	Paste or glue
Braid	Scissors
Sequins	Pinking shears
Beads	Christmas tree garland
Pattern (see page 194)	

> **FAITH CONNECTION**
>
> *Remind the children that in the story of Jesus' birth in the Gospel of Luke, we learn that angels proclaimed the birth of Jesus and sang his praise. Point out that we call these angels* heralds, *which means they are messengers of God. Invite the students to create a craft that represents the herald angels of Christmas.*

Directions:

1. Make and staple a cylinder of cardboard 1½" in diameter, or use a toilet tissue roll.

2. Wrap felt around the cylinder and sew down the center back. Cover at the top and bottom with additional felt and add two lengths of braid to trim the bottom and top.

3. Cut a piece of thin cardboard for wings and halo, using the pattern provided on page 194. Cut out the shape again, using white felt.

4. Cut out the inner circle in brown felt for the halo and trim the edges with pinking shears.

5. Cut a smaller wing shape in peach felt and sew to the white felt shape.

6. Paste the inner halo to the white felt and paste the completed wing and halo shape to the cardboard. Decorate the wings with sequins and beads.

7. Paste the wings behind the body cylinder. Cover half of a 1¾" diameter Styrofoam® plastic ball with gold material for the head. Add 2 half sequins for the eyes and a single sequin for the mouth.

8. Paste the head in front of the halo and surround it with about 4½" of gold Christmas tree garland for hair.

Christmas Angel Patterns

Crown

Grades 4–8

Materials:

Double page from a broadsheet (large format)
newspaper cut square or another thin- to medium-
weight sheet 15–20" square, depending on the size of
head it is to fit

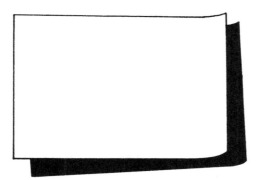

FAITH CONNECTION

*Explain to the children
that the people of Israel,
after being led from
slavery in Egypt to the
Promised Land, asked
for a king to protect
them (see 1 Samuel
8:5). God indeed al-
lowed the people of
Israel to have a king.
Christians see Jesus as
a king whose kingdom
reigns forever and whose
will is to be done on
earth as it is in heaven.
We celebrate the Feast
of Christ the King on
the last Sunday of the
Church year.*

Directions:

1. See the illustrations on pages 196–97. Fold down the center like a book. Unfold.

2. Fold edge AB down to edge CD. (The next drawing is bigger.)

3. Fold edges EA and FB to the center crease. Unfold.

4. Squash fold, bringing A and B to the center crease.

5. Fold C and D behind.

6. Fold in the bottom corners.

7. Then fold up the new corner I.

8. Repeat steps 6 and 7 on the back to make the paper shape symmetrical front and back. (The next drawing is bigger.)

9. Open the pocket along the bottom edge and push down on crease GH.

10. Continue to open the pocket and to flatten the crease against G and H until the crown shape emerges.

11. When the crown is complete, crease down the 4 sides to make it more like a square.

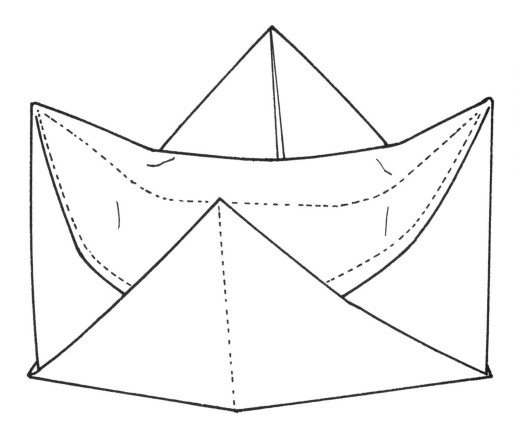

Crown Directions

1.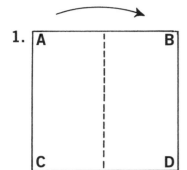

2.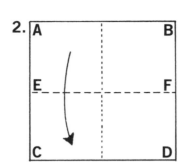

3.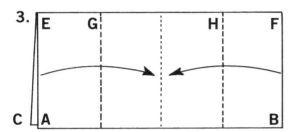

4.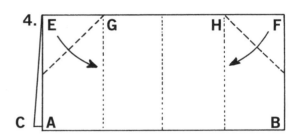

5.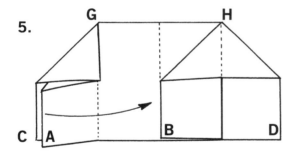

6.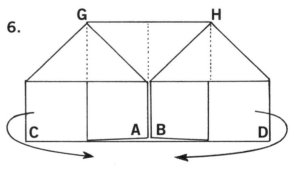

7.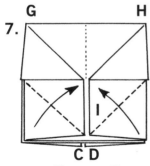

8.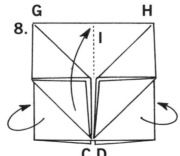

9.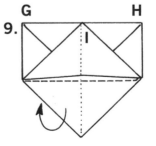

9.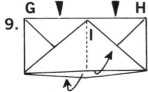

10.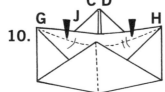

11.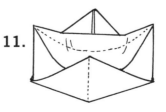

Cycle A, Church: Our Signs

Cycle A, Church: Our Signs concentrates on the seven sacraments and the signs and symbols of each sacrament, which stand for the deeper spiritual reality behind the visible symbol. Explain to the students that we are able to communicate with others by using symbols. Symbols give information about or stand for something more than they are. For example, a clock is a symbol for time, a barber shop pole for hair cutting, clouds for rain, and a heart for love.

One of the earliest symbols used by Christians to represent Jesus Christ is the fish. It was a secret sign for early believers to identify themselves to each other because they were publicly persecuted for their belief in Jesus. The Greek initials for Jesus Christ, *ICHTHUS,* spell out the word *fish* and served as a code to other believers. Various crosses, such as the Jerusalem cross and the Chi-Rho, are also ancient symbols that represent Christ. Other symbols represent the seven sacraments.

Session 1:

Session 2:

Session 3:

Review: You might want to use one of the projects from a previous session that you have not already use.

Cycle B, Church: Our Beliefs

Cycle B, Church: Our Beliefs explores what we as a Church believe and celebrate. The four main beliefs covered here are God, Jesus, Holy Spirit, and Resurrection. Students also study the liturgy of the Church through which these beliefs are celebrated in community.

Three important aspects of faith are (1) God's revelation to us, (2) our response to God's free gift of faith to us, and (3) how we develop our faith in relationship with God, Jesus, and each other. Both the experiential use of symbols and familiar objects from everyday life can be valuable means of expressing a faith that is difficult to define. These craft projects will help to represent symbolically each belief for the students in an enjoyable way.

Session 1:

Session 2:

Session 3:

Session 4:

Session 5:

Session 6:

Session 7:

Session 8:

Review: You might want to use one of the projects from a previous session that you have not already use.

Cycle C, Church: Our Story

Cycle C, Church: Our Story is the story of our religious heritage in the Old Testament, which begins some two thousand years before the coming of Jesus into time. This story begins with an introduction of the patriarchs Abraham and Moses and the establishment of the covenant between God and the Hebrew people. The first kings of the Hebrew nation, King David and King Solomon, are introduced. Fidelity to the covenant is the chief concern of the prophets who, in the person of Jeremiah, remind the kings and people to live by their promises and to act justly.

The mission of Jesus completes the hope of the early covenant. The lifestyle of the first Christians reflects a concern for all members of the community and the just sharing of resources. The structure of the Church developed out of this experience and the growing need to adjust to an expanding Church.

The crafts outlined in this cycle will reinforce the themes to promote a hands-on experience of learning.

Session 5:

Session 6:

If this session is during Lent, you might use a Resurrection or a Prayer project.

Session 7:

Session 8:

Review: You might want to use one of the projects from a previous session that you have not already use.

Cycle D, Church: Our Life

Cycle D, Church: Our Life centers on our responsibility toward each other as members of the Church in the world and on some personalities who influence us as models of the Christian lifestyle. The lifestyle of Jesus demonstrates how the eight Beatitudes and the two greatest commandments to love God and neighbor can lead us to love ourselves in a healthy way and to reach out to others unselfishly.

Mary is presented as the mother of Jesus and mother of the Church. Other saints, such as St. Stephen, the first martyr; St. Francis of Assisi, who founded the Franciscan Order; and St. Elizabeth Ann Seton, as the first American-born saint, are recognized through the process of canonization by the Church to be truly Christian people.

We must remember, however, that there are many other people in every age who love God and have concern for others. Many of the following projects will affirm students in the Christian lifestyle by reinforcing how much they are loved by God.

Review: You might want to use one of the projects from a previous session that you have not already use.

Topical Index

Lent

Love

Alphabetical Index